FESTIVE FLOWERS

FESTIVE FLOWERS

PAULA PRYKE

PHOTOGRAPHY BY **JONATHAN LOVEKIN**

This book is dedicated with gratitude to all the customers and clients
who have supported me through the years

First published in the United States of America in 1997 by
RIZZOLI INTERNATIONAL PUBLICATIONS, INC.
300 Park Avenue South, New York, NY 10010

First published in Great Britain in 1997 by
Mitchell Beazley, an imprint of Reed International Books Limited,
Michelin House, 81 Fulham Road, London SW3 6RB
and Auckland and Melbourne

ISBN 0-8478-2039-4
LC 97-66477

Executive Editor **Judith More**
Executive Art Editor **Janis Utton**
Senior Editor **Jane Struthers**
Design **XAB Design**
Project Editor **Anthea Snow**
Production **Kate Thomas**
Indexer **Ann Barrett**

Printed and bound in China

CONTENTS

INTRODUCTION

Flowers celebrate with us on our birthdays, at anniversaries and at weddings. My most rewarding,

and often most challenging, work as a florist lies in arranging the ordinary day-to-day deliveries of

bouquets and arrangements, sent to mark a simple celebration or a memorable occasion. When you

enter a career in the flower business you become one element of the ups and downs of your customers,

and as they go through life you are often called upon to mark their high points and share their joys.

The most successful celebrations reflect your own style and your generosity of spirit as a host or

hostess – something that is not necessarily dictated either by a tight budget or by flamboyant excess.

We have all enjoyed some simple festivities more than lavish parties because they have embodied the

spirit of a true celebration. When organizing a large celebratory event, I may meet the family several

times during the course of making all the arrangements. By the time the big day comes, I have often

become quite intimate with the grand plan of the day. The successful and happy execution of these

events is both an honour and a joy. I consider myself extremely fortunate to work in a profession that is

rewarding and creative, and allows me to work with beautiful raw materials every day.

PARTIES

I was asked to design a table arrangement incorporating the 'Lilian Baylis' rose (*Rosa*), and chose astrantia (*Astrantia*) and sweet peas (*Lathyrus odoratus*) with a foil of flowery hebe (*Hebe*) and lady's mantle (*Alchemilla mollis*). The cream flowers are complemented by a thick church candle. To anchor this in the middle of each arrangement, four stub wires, bent double, have been secured to the bottom of the candle using green floral foam tape, and then pushed into the middle of the floral foam. To hold the display, an inexpensive florist's container has been covered with strips of double-sided adhesive tape and then glossy laurel (*Laurus*) leaves have been stuck upright around the outside and tied with a hank of raffia.

"Formal parties often involve months of planning. This party marked the temporary closure of the celebrated Sadler's Wells Theatre, in London, for refurbishment. The renowned nursery, R. Harkness & Co., had created a beautiful rose in memory of Lilian Baylis, manager of Sadler's Wells in the 1930s."

ANNIVERSARY PARTY

The romantic celebration of an anniversary is an opportunity to use bold and warm

colours to good advantage. For this ruby wedding party, the colour of the jewel

has been developed into a floral theme of deep pink and purple flowers,

complemented by dark-green foliage.

Above: Kir, a blend of dry white wine and cassis, makes a deliciously refreshing
aperitif and here has the added advantage of matching the party's colour scheme.

Right: Scented 'Jacaranda', 'Stirling Silver' and 'Ecstasy' roses (*Rosa*) are mixed
with spray 'Tamango' roses and deep-purple Mona Lisa anemones (*Anemone*).
Terra-cotta pots have been covered with rich, deep-purple velvet and filled with
brightly coloured flowers to give a warm feel to the winter party.

Above: If you plan to use high containers on stands, you should consider placing a few flowers or petals at the base of each stand to make the table look attractive. Here, three roses (*Rosa*) have been placed in a vial of water hidden in the bottom of the arrangement. However, roses can usually last for an evening without water.

The table decorations and garlands have been swathed in deep-purple velvet and trimmed with gold cord. Half the table decorations are high and half are low, to create added interest. All incorporate thick candles and contain love-lies-bleeding (*Amaranthus*), dark ivy (*Hedera*) trails and long sprigs of maidenhair fern (*Adiantum capillus-veneris*) to give a tumbling effect.

When planning tall table decorations it is always sensible to allow enough height for your guests to be able to see under the arrangement and across the table. Although guests very rarely communicate across a large table that seats twelve, it is friendlier and more intimate if they are able to make eye contact.

Nearby, small blocks of floral foam have been attached to the stair railings using floral foam tape, and have been filled with trailing arrangements. This type of display can be very useful when floor space is limited.

Right: Roses look very romantic by candlelight, and as the heat rises so does their heady scent.

Below: 'Chateaux' gerberas (*Gerbera*) are used in the garlands. Big arrangements call for flowers with plenty of visual impact – small or indistinguished flowers would be lost in a large display. Trailing berried ivy (*Hedera*) and hypericum (*Hypericum*) are among my favourite winter foliages.

Bottom: Lisianthus (*Eustoma*) is such a versatile and popular flower that it is now produced almost all the year round. Trails of lisianthus give a sense of movement to large arrangements.

ENTRANCE FLOWERS

Scent and impact are the two most important factors when choosing entrance

flowers. In a large space, a huge welcoming arrangement helps to break the ice.

Pedestal arrangements are a very useful way to show the flowers at eye level.

If the interior is dark, you should choose flowers that are light in colour.

Above: A birch and moss pedestal urn filled with peonies (*Paeonia*), lilac (*Syringa vulgaris*), delphiniums
(*Delphinium*), foxgloves (*Digitalis*), *Trachelium*, longiflorum lilies (*Lilium longiflorum*), 'Casablanca'
lilies, guelder roses (*Viburnum opulus*), cherry blossom (*Prunus*) and mock orange (*Philadelphus*).

Right: The bottom of a topiary frame has been covered with yarrow (*Achillea millefolium*). The flowers
are *Gloriosa superba*, 'Christian' spray and 'Aalsmeer Gold' roses (*Rosa*), achillea, guelder roses
(*Viburnum opulus*), green dill (*Anethum graveolens*) and love-lies-bleeding (*Amaranthus*).

Placing arrangements on existing furniture, such as console tables, makes them look less contrived. Whenever possible, it is a good idea to use the furniture or vases that already occupy your party space rather than to hire a number of pedestals, as that can overpower the room or make it appear overdressed.

Texture is very important in all my work, and here I have used the very tactile cock's comb (*Celosia*) and leucospermums (*Leucospermum*) to add drama. I have chosen a distinctly multicoloured scheme, using dark-green ruscus (*Ruscus*) and the blue-green spinning gum (*Eucalyptus perriniana*) to tone with the acid colour of the hypericum (*Hypericum*) berries, and the leucospermums to tone with the deep-red cock's comb. The lime-green bells of Ireland (*Molucella laevis*) give form to the arrangement. The 'Monte Negro' lilies (*Lilium*) look wonderful with the deep-mauve delphiniums (*Delphinium*) and the lisianthus (*Eustoma*). I have used the superbly scented 'Ecstasy' and the old-fashioned 'Mainzer Fastnach' roses (*Rosa*) in groups of two to create extra impact.

19

TOPIARY TREE

MATERIALS

Red, yellow and pink cock's
  comb (*Celosia*)
Red 'Salsa' and orange 'Paso'
  germini (*Gerbera*)
'Nicole' roses (*Rosa*)
Florist's knife
Flowerfood solution
Conical topiary tree frame
Large ceramic pot
Sphagnum moss
1-inch (2.5cm) gauge wire
  mesh, large enough to wrap
  around the topiary frame
Heavy-gauge florist's reel wire
Length of burgundy silk, long
  enough to wind around the
  topiary frame several times
Heavy stub wires
Bunch of 0.20mm silver wires
Red chili peppers (*Capsicum*)
Mauve peppers (*Capsicum*)
Orange peppers
Purple aubergines (*Solanum*)

The inspiration for this
arrangement came from a
corporate retirement party
with an Indian theme. Strong
colours were used throughout
the restaurant, and peppers,
aubergines and chilies all
featured on the menu as well
as in the decorations. Fruits
and vegetables are excellent
for large displays because they
are dramatic, colourful and
less expensive than flowers.

1 Work on a flat, non-scratch
and waterproof surface, or
cover the work surface with
plastic sheeting. Condition
the flowers well by trimming
at least 1 inch (2.5cm) off the
bottom of each stem with the
florist's knife and leaving the
flowers in a solution of
flowerfood for 24 hours.
Place the topiary tree frame
on top of the ceramic pot.

2 Pack the topiary tree frame
with damp sphagnum moss
until it is firm. If the moss has
dried out, spray it with water
before using it.

3 Cover the frame with
1-inch (2.5cm) wire mesh
and tightly bind it in place
with heavy-gauge florist's reel
wire. Work from the top of
the frame to the bottom and
secure the ends of the wire
neatly and firmly.

4 Arrange the burgundy silk
in a spiral around the frame,
anchoring it at the top and
bottom with heavy stub wires
bent double to form hairpins.
    Cut off the heads of the
cock's comb and the roses,
leaving 1½ inches (3.5cm) of
stem, and attach a double-leg
mount to each. To do this,
bend double a heavy stub
wire and place the U-shaped
end of the wire against the
cut-off stem. Twist one half of
the double-leg around the
other. This method extends the
stem by giving it two wire legs.
    Cut off the heads of the
germini, leaving 1½ inches
(3.5cm) of stem. Give the
germini internal wires (see
page 68) and then double-leg
mounts. Begin to spear the
flowers into the topiary tree.
    Wire the chilies in groups
by threading several at a time
with a stub wire and then
twisting the two ends of wire
together. Wire the peppers by
pushing a stub wire through
the flesh of each and then
twisting the wire ends together.
The aubergines may have to
be held in place with two stub
wires. To do this, push one
stub wire through the flesh and
another wire at right angles to
the first one. Twist the wire
ends together. Begin to spear
the chilies, peppers and
aubergines into the tree.

You can create a rich textural effect by arranging the germinis, roses and cock's comb in groups of three around the topiary frame (*right*), and by placing the chilies in clusters. To give a vivid effect, place contrasting colours and textures next to one another. Continue to place the flowers and vegetables around the cone until you can no longer see any gaps or wire mesh.

Left: For increased impact, the flowers and foliage have been arranged in groups. They include 'Nicole', 'Bahama' and 'Renate' roses (*Rosa*), green dill (*Anethum graveolens*), hypericum (*Hypericum*) berries, alliums (*Allium*), Jerusalem sage (*Phlomis fruticosa*), 'Centura' and 'Tennessee' gerberas (*Gerbera*) and blackberries (*Rubus fruticosus*). Stripped honeysuckle vine (*Lonicera*) swirls from the top of the container to the base flowers to connect the two sections of the arrangement.

Right: To create a Venetian theme, a bold candelabra is covered with gold leaf and dressed with a commedia dell'arte papier-mâché mask. Dark-red cotinus (*Cotinus*) foliage creates a dramatic foil for the peach 'Renate' and dark-red 'Nicole' roses (*Rosa*), green dill (*Anethum graveolens*), hebe (*Hebe*) flowers and glory lilies (*Gloriosa superba*).

TALL TABLE ARRANGEMENTS

Tall table displays can add an element of height to a room. Wreath-frames are ideal for covering the mechanics at the base, which must be heavy to ensure stability, and the frames allow flowers to fit in floral foam rather than rest on the table.

FORMAL URN DISPLAY

MATERIALS

Hebe (*Hebe*)

Lady's mantle (*Alchemilla mollis*)

White ranunculus (*Ranunculus*)

'Doris Rijkers' roses (*Rosa*)

Peach sweet peas (*Lathyrus odorata*)

Small sunflowers (*Helianthus*)

Large variegated ivy (*Hedera*) leaves

Variegated pittosporum (*Pittosporum*)

Viburnum (*Viburnum*) berries

Florist's knife

Flowerfood solution

1 block of floral foam

1 9-inch (17.5cm) diameter rusty urn

1 black plastic sheet

Handful of sphagnum moss

Florist's scissors

Urns look good at formal parties and these miniature, rusty table urns make perfect table centres because they are heavy and stable. Spray paint is the easiest way to transform urns, but paint finishes of all types can be used as a camouflage or to give them a different look – one of my favourites is a verdigris effect.

1 Work on a flat, non-scratch and waterproof surface, or cover the work surface with plastic sheeting. Condition the flowers and foliage (see page 20). Soak the floral foam in a solution of flowerfood until air bubbles no longer rise to the surface. Do not force the foam under water because this will cause air locks. Leave it floating on the surface and wait until it soaks up enough water to become submerged. It is now completely saturated and ready to use.

2 Line the urn with the plastic sheet. Cut the floral foam to fit the lined urn so that the foam sits substantially above the edge, to give the finished arrangement a domed effect. Place the foam firmly in position and trim off all the hard edges with the knife, so that you can insert the flowers at an angle. Arrange sphagnum moss between the foam and the lining to conceal the plastic. Using the scissors, trim the ivy leaf stems with a slanting cut, to expose the maximum amount of surface area to the moisture in the foam. Place the ivy leaves around the edge of the urn to hide the foam.

3 Arrange groups of foliage to cover the floral foam. I always like to use a variety of foliages to create a natural look and add texture, and I use berries if they are in season. If you pick plant material from your garden you can use different seed heads, and can even incorporate imperfect flowers as a foil to your other blooms. For instance, sunflower petals can be damaged by the weather but the central seed disc alone looks attractive.

When you have created a good rounded shape with the foliage, start to arrange the flowers in groups (*right*). Begin with the roses because these have the strongest stems, then add the ranunculus. Add the sweet peas last because they have the weakest stems. When arranging sweet peas in floral foam, place your hand very close to the foam and gently slide in each stem, guiding it with your fingers.

CLASSICAL CANDELABRA

MATERIALS

'Orlando' lilies (*Lilium*)
Love-lies-bleeding
    (*Amaranthus*)
'Karl Rosenfeld' peonies
    (*Paeonia*)
'Duchesse de Nemours'
    peonies
'Ecstasy' roses (*Rosa*)
'Salal' gaultheria (*Gaultheria
    shallon*)
Ivy (*Hedera*) trails
Guelder roses (*Viburnum
    opulus*)
Soft ruscus (*Ruscus racemosa*)
    leaves
'Snowmound' spirea (*Spiraea
    nipponica*)
'Foliis Purpureis' weigela
    (*Weigela florida*)
Florist's knife
Flowerfood solution
Sturdy candelabra
2 blocks of floral foam
2-inch (5cm) gauge wire
    mesh, large enough to cover
    the blocks of floral foam
Heavy-gauge florist's reel wire
Candles

If you are often asked to decorate using candelabra, it is a good idea to have some made to your own design. You can then create a dish in which to place the floral foam with sufficient space to allow you to water the foam and therefore keep the arrangement moist longer. I have a number of candelabra, some free-standing and some suitable for tables; there are even hanging versions.

1 Work on a flat, non-scratch and waterproof surface, or cover the work surface with plastic sheeting. Condition the flowers and foliage (see page 20). Stand the candelabra upright. Soak the floral foam in a solution of flowerfood (see page 24), then cut it into three or four large pieces and place these around the central candle holder. (This candelabra was specially made for displaying flowers, but you can wire or tape the blocks around the central candle holder of a standard candelabra.) Wrap the wire mesh around the foam and secure it with lengths of reel wire, making sure that the ends of the wires are not visible.

2 Place the foliage around the candelabra, using the natural shape of each item to create a soft, flowing look. Some foliages, such as the guelder roses and the weigela, naturally droop and so are ideal for this sort of arrangement. 'Salal' gaultheria is a good filler because of its large leaves.

3 Add the roses at different heights and depths around the arrangement. 'Ecstasy' roses are a dark, velvety red and have the beautiful scent of garden roses. Add the love-lies-bleeding and the peonies.

4 Place the single lily heads around the arrangement at different heights. The very wide, star-shaped face of the hybrid lily 'Orlando' has been specially developed for large arrangements: it has a single head on a long stem, with no other buds or branches. Check the arrangement for gaps, then add the candles (*right*), taking care not to damage the flowers.

The increasingly popular trend of holding weddings and blessings outside traditional buildings such as churches, synagogues and town halls has expanded the floral opportunities for weddings. Here, an old French metal bench has been rubbed down, painted with red oxide, coated with gold paint and then trails of silvery Canary Island ivy (*Hedera canariensis* 'Gloire de Marengo'), which have been wired into a heart shape, were attached to it. Inside the heart sit two tied swags of beautiful 'Anna' standard roses (*Rosa*) and spray 'Diadeen' roses with lisianthus (*Eustoma*), trimmed with scented, variegated geranium leaves (*Pelargonium crispum* 'Variegatum').

SUMMER PARASOL

MATERIALS

Foxgloves (*Digitalis*)

'Orlando' lilies (*Lilium*)

Double lisianthus (*Eustoma russellıanum*)

Love-lies-bleeding (*Amaranthus*)

Mock orange (*Philadelphus*)

'Sarah Bernhardt' peonies (*Paeonia*)

Snapdragons (*Anthirrhinum*)

Lady fern (*Athyrium filix-femina*)

Variegated 'Drummondii' maple (*Acer platanoides*)

Crossed-leafed orach (*Atriplex*)

Guelder roses (*Viburnum opulus*)

Florist's knife

Flowerfood solution

Plastic sheeting

2 floral foam rackets

Garden parasol

Floral foam tape

Parasol-type marquees are often supported by poles running through the middles of tables, which prevents you from creating traditional table centres. Instead, you can decorate the frame that joins the top of the pole with the underside of the canvas, or place a wreath frame around the hole in the table.

1 Condition the flowers and foliage (see page 20). Cover the table and floor with plastic sheeting. Rackets, with their cage of plastic and a handle attached, were originally developed for sympathy work. I like to use them in hanging arrangements such as this one because they help to keep the floral foam intact. Soak the rackets in a solution of flowerfood (see page 24), then attach them back-to-back to the top of the parasol frame using plenty of floral foam tape.

2 Start by following the line of the parasol with long pieces of foliage in order to establish the shape. At first the floral foam will drip water, but this will soon stop. In the meantime, keep the arrangement away from anything that will be spoiled by the leaking water.

3 When you have covered the floral foam with foliage, you can begin to add the flowers. The shape and length of the snapdragons makes them ideal for defining the points of this arrangement, and the trailing love-lies-bleeding creates a flowing effect.

4 Add the foxgloves at different heights, some following the line of the parasol and some pointing toward the table below. The fluffy peonies and the large 'Orlando' lilies are marvellous focal flowers. If you are using lilies in an overhead arrangement it is a good idea to remove the stamens first – this prevents any allergy problems and also stops the pollen from dropping and staining whatever it lands on. To do this, carefully nip out the stamens with your fingers, then wash your hands to avoid spreading the pollen to other flowers or your clothes. Finally, add the lisianthus.

"The budget for informal parties

can be a major consideration, so

I often recommend to customers

that we create maximum impact

with one spectacular arrangement

rather than use several smaller

ones. A tall container is great for

parties where most of the guests

will be standing, because the

flowers will be at eye level."

The look of a party is enhanced by matching the presentation of the food to the flowers. Small sprigs of blossom and herbs make canapés look more attractive: snake grass (*Scirpus tabernaemontani* 'Zebrinus') is perfect for smoked salmon parcels tied up with chives. Larger leaves and reeds make an ideal lining for a tray or plate: banana tree leaves are harvested in Thailand, the leaves cut into two and the central vein removed; they are then used around the world for displaying food. Many flowerheads are edible and a number of countries, including Israel, are increasingly producing flowerheads such as pansy (*Viola*) and nasturtium (*Tropaeolum*) purely for the presentation of food or for incorporating in salads. Make sure that you wash all plant material before putting it near food.

Recently there has been a fashion to use fruits and vegetables in floral decorations, and consequently vegetables are sold through the flower markets. Globe artichokes (*Cynara scolymus*) and members of the *Brassica oleracea* family, such as cabbages, Brussels sprouts and cauliflowers, are particularly decorative in place of other foliage.

THANKSGIVING

Although Thanksgiving is considered a typically American celebration, thanksgiving

festivals around the world are as old as recorded history. Most are based on a

successful harvest: in China, the Moon Festival celebrates the harvest with moon-

shaped cakes and candies; in Austria, 15 November is known as St Leopold's Day or

"Goose Day", when dishes of goose are eaten to celebrate the new wine season.

Above: Cooked pumpkin is often seasoned with sugar and spices, but pumpkin
needs few additions when used as a decoration because of its wonderful
markings and spectacular colours.

Right: An ancient water-wheel makes the perfect support for a thick garland of
hops (*Humulus lupulus*), hydrangea heads (*Hydrangea*), grapevines (*Vitis vinifera*),
cotinus (*Cotinus*) and love-lies-bleeding (*Amaranthus*). Sunflowers (*Helianthus*),
apples, gourds, pumpkins and berried cotoneaster (*Cotoneaster*) add colour.

The large pedestal arrangement (*left*) uses groups of yellow foxtail lilies (*Eremurus*) and sunflowers (*Helianthus*). The orange colouring of the 'Monte Negro' lilies (*Lilium*) and berried cotoneaster (*Cotoneaster*) add warmth and contrast with the dark-purple sprays of cotinus (*Cotinus*). Chinese lanterns (*Physalis*) give an attractive autumnal effect. The other foliage includes trails of ivy (*Hedera*) and grapevines (*Vitis vinifera*).

Black grapes, which echo the colour of the cotinus in the pedestal arrangement, are used in the table centres. Apples are also used. When wiring both these fruits into arrangements, it looks attractive to display them with the stalks showing. Fruit always looks good in arrangements but it is not practical for displays that are intended to last for several days because the ethylene gas that it produces can hasten the deterioration of the flowers.

If you are incorporating candles in your display, never leave them unattended when lit. Instead of placing candles within an arrangement, you can circle it with them held in safe glass-covered or ceramic containers.

Above: Any large arrangement requires flowers and foliages with different shapes. *Eremurus* lends height and a feathery quality. Adding fruit and vegetables creates texture as well as colour. By using vines bearing fruit, the arrangement incorporates elements of the harvest itself.

Right: The feathery 'Aalsmeer Gold' rose (*Rosa*) grouped with love-lies-bleeding (*Amaranthus*) and *Hypericum* berries.

Below: When hollowed out and lined with sheets of black plastic, giant pumpkins make excellent containers. Here, candles sit with 'Royale' and 'Leonotus' roses (*Rosa*), 'Festival' lilies (*Lilium*), leucadendron 'Safari Sunset' (*Leucadendron*), copper beech (*Fagus*), hypericum (*Hypericum*) and green dill (*Anethum graveolens*).

Bottom: 'Leonotus' roses (*Rosa*) are the latest in a family of two-tone roses.

ARRANGEMENTS WITH IMPACT

Contemporary interiors with minimal decoration suit arrangements with an
emphasis on bold forms, clean lines and crisply defined colours. In such architectural
displays, the choice of container is as important as the flowers to the overall effect.

Above: Mung beans have been glued onto balls of dried floral foam, and cloves and star anise have
been pushed into green floral foam balls. The flowers are 'Mona Lisa' anemones (*Anemone*) and
'Stirling Silver' roses (*Rosa*). The foliage is rosemary (*Rosmarinus*), camellia (*Camellia*) leaves, cardoon
heads (*Cynara cardunculus*), sea holly (*Eryngium*) and purple poppy seed heads (*Papaver*).

Right: The vase is edged with pompon moss. Contrasting dark-purple and bright-yellow arum lilies
(*Zantedeschia*) are topped by allium heads (*Allium christophii*).

INFORMAL ARRANGEMENTS

Even the most informal parties benefit from a few carefully chosen flower
arrangements. You can select simple, vividly coloured flowers for a
children's birthday party, or experiment with flowers, foliage and unusual
containers for a more sophisticated event.

Above: Although as a young girl I spent many hours picking wild flowers, a great
number of them are now protected because they are so rare, and should be left
to re-seed and multiply. This woodland arrangement uses forest ferns (*Dryopteris
filix-mas*), foxgloves (*Digitalis*) and dock (*Rumex thyrsiflora*).

Right: By placing a narrow cylinder inside a wide one, you can create two spaces
to fill. Here, one contains jelly beans for a children's party. Later, the inner vase of
zinnias (*Zinnia*) can be removed and the bright sweets can be bagged up.

SEASHORE TABLE CENTRE

MATERIALS

'Bianca' roses (*Rosa*)

Spider fern (*Pteris multifida*)

Proteas (*Protea pityphylla*)

'Orion' sea holly (*Eryngium maritimum*)

White trachelium (*Trachelium caeruleum* 'Album')

Florist's knife

Flowerfood solution

1 block of floral foam

Low, organic-shaped pottery dish

Green floral foam tape

Selection of shells

Driftwood

Bunch of heavy stub wires

Coral fan or large shell

Pompon moss

Starfish or large shell

Long walks on beaches often provide a real treasure trove of shells and driftwood that can add interest to informal arrangements. Many dried-flower suppliers hold stocks of items, but there is nothing so rewarding as incorporating your own mementoes collected on holiday.

1 Work on a flat, non-scratch and waterproof surface, or cover the work surface with plastic sheeting. Condition the flowers and foliage (see page 20). It is important to choose a container that suits your style of arrangement. This hand-made bowl is like an open oyster shell, making it the ideal choice for a natural, organic table centre. Shells that you have collected can be used time and time again.

2 Cut the block of floral foam to fit the bowl, then soak it in a solution of flowerfood (see page 24). Place the foam in the bowl and secure it with two strips of floral foam tape arranged in a cross. (Floral foam tape is available in three colours and several widths. The dark-green, thin tape used here is the most versatile. The white tape is useful with white ceramic bowls and when using white tablecloths.

It is often used in wedding work. The brown tape combines well with dried flowers, and is the same colour as brown dried floral foam.) Arrange the shells around the edges of the bowl and through the middle of the arrangement. These can be secured by spearing them in the floral foam as shown. Place the driftwood through the arrangement and secure it using heavy stub wires bent double to form hairpins.

3 Add the fan of coral. It is increasingly difficult to buy coral and you should never collect it from the sea yourself as it is now a protected species. This is a piece that I have had for many years. If you cannot find any coral, you could use an attractive shell instead. Now add sprigs of the pompon moss, sprigs of the spider fern and the sea holly, until the foam is completely covered.

4 Add the white trachelium as a filler, followed by the proteas. Place the starfish or one large shell in the middle of the arrangement as a focal point. Finally, place the 'Bianca' roses at different heights in a zigzag effect across the arrangement.

WEDDINGS

"I love designing wedding

celebrations as each one is

unique. There is something very

refreshing and exciting about

the anticipation of the wedding,

and working closely with a

family to create someone's

dream day."

Bridal bouquets are the floral centrepiece of the wedding and many factors combine to determine the final look: the size of the bride, the style of her dress, the colour scheme and, of course, her favourite flowers.

Some brides have unrealistic expectations of what they can choose. One bride came to me wanting white camellias (*Camellia*) in the middle of summer, a time when they are not available in Britain. In fact, even in spring they are in scant supply and difficult to order in one colour. If you are desperate to have a certain flower then it is important to plan your day when it is in season. Modern hybridization and worldwide transportation means that you can have almost anything that you want at any time, but at a higher cost than if you select flowers in season. My advice is always to make your choice according to season, so that you get the best value and can have the greatest number of blooms.

MARQUEE RECEPTION

The marquee is a popular way of extending your family home or garden for a large party. It is also an opportunity to use a grand garden or historical site for your reception. Marquees differ enormously – from basic canvas tents to versions with ruched silk interiors and French doors.

Above: Traditional gifts for wedding guests, known as "favours", were often twists of sugared almonds wrapped in tulle. Recently it has become popular to place a disposable camera on each table; here, it is accompanied by the gift of an album.

Right: Sophisticated cream settings have been brightened by the scented summer flowers. The table centres vary but the same flowers have been used throughout to complement the wedding theme.

Once you have chosen your marquee, the supplier will provide you with a table plan and from this you can work out the most suitable sites for floral decorations. Traditional frame tents usually have two supporting poles, which look wonderful wrapped with a spiral of flowers and foliage. For weddings, you must make sure that all the flowers are fully open to create maximum impact, so avoid choosing flowers that are still in tight bud unless you are buying them a few days early.

If you are planning an event using a caterer, there is much more scope for you to be involved in the complete look of the party – you can choose your own cutlery, china and tableware. Most caterers hire all these items for each event from specialist companies, so the choice can be very wide. Although coloured tablecloths and brightly coloured china can give an event a strong personality, it is worth bearing in mind that often food looks best served on plain white china. For this wedding, a gold theme has been carried through the decorations, from the elegant chairs to the gilt-edged china and glass.

Above: These tall candelabras are excellent for giving height and filling a large space. They also have the advantage of allowing guests to talk across the table because they are high enough to give an uninterrupted view. When choosing candles, it is important to select types that burn very slowly, such as church candles.

Right: A floral foam ring has been placed around the base of each candelabra to create a low-grouped arrangement. The middle has been filled with grapes surrounded by Poppy (*Papaver*) seed heads, 'La Minuet' roses (*Rosa*), candytuft (*Iberis*), *Eryngium*, *Alchemilla mollis* and sweet peas (*Lathyrus odoratus*).

Below and bottom: For this wedding, the bride chose a cream marquee, with gilt touches, as a neutral background for the brightly coloured flower arrangements. This suits a lunchtime summer party where the overall impression is fresh and light.

The decorations for any ceremony need to be considered with care, and for Jewish celebrations the chuppah is the focus of the whole wedding. A couple can get married anywhere, provided the ceremony is held under the chuppah. This enables many Jewish weddings to take place outdoors in splendid weather. For those who marry in a synagogue, the four poles holding the canopy of the chuppah are usually decorated with flowers. Either the tops of the poles are decorated or the decorations hang down to the floor, for which rackets (blocks of floral foam within a plastic frame) are fixed to the chuppah poles with reel wire or floral foam tape.

"Decorating the chuppah can be

quite a complicated procedure.

It usually requires specific

timing for both the installation

and removal of the flowers to be

possible on a single day, so it is

advisable to use a professional

florist for synagogue decoration."

WINTER WEDDING

Whenever possible I like to use seasonal foliage. The availability of commercially grown berried foliage, wonderful in autumn and winter wedding arrangements, has significantly increased over the last decade or so because flower-growers all over the world have produced new varieties and revived old favourites.

Above: It is a lovely idea to have natural confetti. Here, I have trimmed a heart-shaped twig basket with orange freesias (*Freesia*) and variegated ivy (*Hedera*), then filled it with rose (*Rosa*) petal confetti.

Left: Boughs of blackberries (*Rubus fruticosus*), elderflowers (*Sambucus*) and tendrils of old man's beard (*Clematis vitalba*), all of which are beautiful fillers, with Hypericum (*Hypericum*), which is now sold throughout the year. 'Golden Charmer' pyracantha (*Pyracantha*) has vivid orange berries and picks up the arum lilies (*Zantedeschia*).

When deciding which area of a church to decorate, it is essential to consider the scale of the building. Lack of space in small churches makes pew-end and pedestal arrangements impractical. Instead, decorations are best placed in the windows or hung onto screens. Large churches look good when decorated with one or two substantial displays, or when decorations are placed high up on columns, around the pulpit or upper chancel. For a grander effect, you can decorate doorways and lych-gates with swags.

It is important to find out whether you are the only couple to be married on your wedding day, and to discuss your proposed decorations with the priest or verger. Most churches are delighted to have plenty of decorations but some prefer to restrict the amount of flowers. You should also ask if paper confetti is permitted – if not, you could use fresh rose petals.

Above: Most country churches were at first largely funded by a wealthy local family, who created their own raised seating area, called a "box", so that the villagers could look up to them on Sundays. In this tiny church we have decorated the two wooden sconces in front of the box.

Right: The bouquet contains 'Leonotus' roses (*Rosa*), 'Maggi Oei' Singapore orchids (*Dendrobium*) and burnt-orange arum lilies (*Zantedeschia*), trimmed with hypericum (*Hypericum*) foliage and galax (*Galax*) leaves.

Below: The rural theme is given a rich touch by spraying montbretia (*Crocosmia*) seed heads gold so that they shine like jewels.

Bottom: The keyholder of the church has raised money for its upkeep by selling her excellent home-made jams, jellies and marmalades.

BRIDAL BOUQUETS

The major determining factor when choosing the bridal bouquet's shape and style is the design and appearance of the wedding dress. After the shape has been decided upon, the colour and variety of flowers are selected. The bride usually chooses her favourite flowers, and fragrance is always paramount.

Above: Dusty pink 'Black Tea' roses (*Rosa*) are toned with burgundy arum lilies (*Zantedeschia*). Burgundy orach (*Atriplex*) seed heads are contrasted with white dill (*Ammi majus*) and 'Salal' gaultheria (*Gaultheria shallon*).

Right: Dark-red 'Peter Brand' peonies (*Paeonia*), 'Red Velvet' and 'Tamango' spray roses (*Rosa*) are trimmed with variegated hosta (*Hosta*) leaves. Peonies are immensely popular and a great favourite with brides.

TIED BRIDAL BOUQUET

MATERIALS

'Santini' spray
   chrysanthemums
   (*Chrysanthemum*)
Euphorbia (*Euphorbia fulgens*)
'Festival' lilies (*Lilium*)
Marigolds (*Calendula
   officinalis*)
'Nicole' roses (*Rosa*)
'Papillion' roses
Bear grass (*Dasylirion*)
Green dill (*Anethum
   graveolens*)
Hypericum (*Hypericum*)
Leucadendron (*Leucadendron*)
Tassel bush (*Garrya elliptica*)
Florist's knife
Flowerfood solution
Long plastic tie or string
Florist's scissors
Ribbon

This style of bouquet suits informal weddings. It is also an excellent way of maintaining a bouquet in humid and hot conditions as the flowers can be kept in water for the maximum length of time, and is ideal for brides travelling with their flowers.

1 Work on a flat, non-scratch and waterproof surface, or cover the work surface with plastic sheeting. Condition the flowers and foliage (see page 20). I have chosen the tassel bush for its trailing catkins and the leucadendron for its upright spikes. The hypericum, with its berries, gives another texture. Bear grass creates a wild and natural "freshly picked" look.

2 Remove all the leaves from the flower and foliage stems, using the knife on the harder branches. You must also de-thorn the roses. To do this, slide the knife down each stalk, working away from your body, gently prizing the thorns from the stem without damaging it.

3 Arrange the foliage, except for the dill, to establish a flat, three-dimensional diamond shape. Gather the stems in a spiral so that the point where you hold them is the narrowest. Use the tall, thin leucadendrons to give the bouquet some definition and the hypericum as a tiller. Place branches of the tassel bush and the bear grass through the bouquet.

4 You may find that it helps to use a mirror as you work, so that you can see how the bouquet will look when carried. Place the trailing euphorbia throughout the bouquet. Pinch out the stamens from the lilies (they can stain the dress), then arrange the lilies through the bouquet as the focal flowers. Place the chrysanthemum stems deep into the bouquet to give a rich colouring. Add the 'Papillion' roses diagonally through the bouquet.

Add the dill, the 'Nicole' roses and the marigolds (*right*). Make sure that you keep to the original flat diamond shape. Before you tie the bouquet, check that the bride's end of the bouquet is full and that some flowers are at 45 degrees to the upright ones. Tie the stems securely at the binding point with a plastic tie or string. Trim the stems with the florist's scissors and then cover this area with a ribbon in a complementary colour.

Delicate posies can be arranged in satin handbags for small bridal attendants. The blue bag is filled with lily-of-the-valley (*Convallaria majalis*) and 'Bianca' roses (*Rosa*). The orange bag is simply filled with 'Confetti' roses, while the white bag holds an early-spring mixture of hellebores (*Helleborus*), guelder roses (*Viburnum opulus*), white 'Princess' spray roses and variegated pittosporum (*Pittosporum*).

BRIDESMAID'S POSY

MATERIALS

Lily-of-the-valley (*Convallaria majalis*)

Florist's knife

Flowerfood solution

Thin gold reel wire

Florist's scissors

Dried hojas (*Hojas*) leaves, or fresh galax (*Galax*) or ivy (*Hedera*) leaves, or skeletonized leaves

Lily-of-the-valley (*Convallaria majalis*) is one of the most popular wedding flowers. I have the sweetest childhood memories of visiting a great-aunt and being given posies of freshly-gathered lily-of-the-valley by her neighbour, who had the most perfect, rambling cottage garden.

1 Work on a flat, non-scratch and waterproof surface, or cover the work surface with plastic sheeting. Condition the flowers (see page 20). Lily-of-the-valley is now available all year because the flowers are grown under glass. However, these blooms are sold by the stem and are extremely expensive. Even when in their natural season they are quite scarce and costly, but their attractiveness and scent more than make up for this.

2 Begin to spiral the lily-of-the-valley into a posy. Gather several stems in your hand as a starting point, arranging them to form a spiral. This means that the point where you hold the stems is the narrowest. It allows you to use

more plant material than can usually be held in the hand, and fans out the flowers in a rounded shape. If you need to put down the posy it will remain intact because of the spiralled stems.

3 Continue to add the flowers until you are happy with the bouquet's shape and size, then tie the binding point with the delicate gold wire. Fasten the ends neatly and trim them with the scissors.

4 Use the gold wire to bind the dried hojas leaves carefully around the bouquet, overlapping them as shown. If you prefer, you could use fresh galax (*Galax*) or ivy (*Hedera*) leaves, or skeletonized leaves from the garden – their delicate appearance is ideal for a wedding. Complete the bouquet (*right*) by carefully moulding the final dried leaf into a cone shape and attaching it around the lily-of-the-valley stems so that they are hidden. Bind the leaf and stems tightly with the gold wire, then finish off neatly with the scissors.

BUTTONHOLES
AND RING-BEARERS

Buttonholes are usually supplied with pins; if you are making your own, choose the

pearl-headed type of pin sold by most haberdashery or notions stores. Bear in mind

that light fabrics can be dragged down by the weight of the flowers.

Above: A bun-moss cushion with a silver cord edge and a heart of chincherinchee (*Ornithogalum thyrsoides*) flowerheads for carrying the rings.

Right, clockwise from top left: Germini (*Gerbera*) with grasses and *Gaultheria shallon* leaves; 'La Minuet' rose (*Rosa*) with *Eryngium* and ivy (*Hedera*); *Bouvardia* and ivy; double lisianthus (*Eustoma*) and ivy; arum lily (*Zantedeschia*) with 'Golden Shower' *Oncidium*; 'Bianca' rose with *Viburnum opulus* berries; 'Red Velvet' roses, *Dendrobium* 'James Storei', *Hypericum* and ivy.

ZINNIA CIRCLET

MATERIALS

Zinnias (*Zinnia*)

Hypericum (*Hypericum*) berries

Green ivy (*Hedera*) leaves

Florist's knife

Flowerfood solution

Florist's scissors

Bunch of 0.20mm silver wires

Bunch of 0.71mm florist's
   wires 14 inches (36cm) long

Green gutta percha (This is a
   tape with a rubbery texture
   that grips the wires and
   stretches slightly when it is
   wound around stems and
   squeezed between the
   fingers. Green, white and
   brown tapes are available.)

Before you decide on the bridesmaid's circlet, it is essential to take into account her size, height and colouring, and the fabric of her dress.

1 Work on a flat, non-scratch and waterproof surface, or cover the work surface with plastic sheeting. Condition the flowers and foliage (see page 20). Using the scissors, cut off the flowerheads in preparation for wiring, leaving ¾ of an inch (2cm) of stem. Zinnias are very delicate and so need to be wired at the last minute. Their hollow stems make them vulnerable to harsh treatment.

2 For the wiring, take each ivy leaf and "stitch" a fine silver wire through the central vein on the underside of the leaf. Bend the two wire ends together and twist them to form a long leg that extends past the end of the stem.

Give each of the hypericum stems a double-leg mount, following the method described on page 20 and using the 0.71mm florist's wires.

Give the zinnias internal wires. To do this, insert a silver wire straight up each stem and out through the head, and then bend the end into a hook. Pull the hook downward so that it is embedded in the petals. Thread a second silver wire through the base of the calyx and then twist it around the first silver wire.

3 After you have wired all the leaves, berries and flowers, cover the stems with gutta percha. To do this, hold the tape between your thumb and forefinger and turn it around the wired stem.

4 Bind together two florist's wires to make the frame of the circlet, then cover them with gutta percha. Starting at one end, place the first leaf and flower on the frame so that the flower overlaps the leaf, then tape them into position. Continue taping material onto the frame, alternating the leaves, berries and flowers, so that they sit very close together. Make sure that the shape is full and rounded and that the colours are mixed. Cut off all the spare wires to reduce the weight of the circlet. When you have completed the ring, gently manipulate the flowers so that they are all facing out from the circlet (*right*).

PEW-END AND HANGING DESIGNS

Church furniture and fixtures are precious, so you have to be resourceful when

positioning decorations. If pews have carved ends, you can often tie decorations

onto these, and sometimes you can use fixings left over from previous weddings.

Above: This swag contains double 'Teddy Bear' sunflowers (*Helianthus annus*),
Dahlia 'Corona', *Hypericum* berries, *Crocosmia* seed heads, green dill (*Anethum graveolens*) and periwinkle trails (*Vinca major* 'Variegata').

Right: A bell-shaped twig base has been decorated with periwinkle (*Vinca major* 'Variegata'), *Brunnera macrophylla* 'Dawson's White' and 'King' spray roses (*Rosa*). The roses sit in tiny vials of water hidden among the periwinkle leaves.

BRIDAL BOWER

MATERIALS

Flowers and foliage

Burnt orange arum lilies
(*Zantedeschia*)
'Shamrock' chrysanthemums
(*Chrysanthemum*)
'Festival' lilies (*Lilium*)
'Red discolour' leucadendron
(*Leucadendron*)
'Newton's' leucospermum
(*Leucospermum*)
Montbretia (*Crocosmia*)
Red-hot pokers (*Kniphofia*)
Sunflowers (*Helianthus*)
Yarrow (*Achillea millefolium*)
Box (*Buxus sempervirens*)
Cotoneaster (*Cotoneaster*)
Green dill (*Anethum
graveolens*)
'Salal' gaultheria (*Gaultheria
shallon*)
Mountain ash (*Sorbus
aucuparia*)
Smilax (*Smilax*)
Florist's knife
Flowerfood solution
Plastic sheeting
Bunch of heavy stub wires

Frame

2 square terra-cotta pots
2 smaller plastic buckets
1 garden arch frame
1-inch (2.5cm) gauge wire
mesh, long enough to cover
the length of the frame and
double its width
Sphagnum moss
Heavy-gauge florist's reel wire
Garden hose

There is no better way to
frame an entrance or to create
a flowery bower for wedding
photography than by using a
garden arch or gazebo. Strong
flowers, such as the ones
chosen for this arch, will last
for several days in water-
soaked sphagnum moss.

1 Condition the flowers
and foliage (see page 20).
Cover the floor with plastic
sheeting to protect it. Place
the two plastic buckets inside
the two terra-cotta pots. Firmly
fit the garden arch frame into
the two pots, making sure that
it is sturdy and secure. Make
a thin "scarf" of sphagnum
moss by bending the wire
mesh in half widthways and
filling it with the moss, then
stitching the edges together
with the reel wire.

2 Attach the sphagnum and
mesh "scarf" to the two edges
of the frame with reel wire at
strategic points, making sure
that it fits the frame snugly. You
can now water the frame with
a hose to make sure that the
moss is full of moisture. For
obvious reasons, you should
do this outside, in a place
where the water will drain
away easily. Fill the buckets
inside each terra-cotta pot
with water.

3 Trim the stems of the foliage
and then wire it into bundles,
each one about the size of
your hand, with double-leg
mounts (see page 20). Push
the foliage bundles into the
moss, bending the wire legs
back on themselves to secure
the foliage in place. Make
sure that you mix the foliage
on both sides of the arch to
give an even, textured look.
When you have covered
all the sphagnum moss and
can no longer see any wire
mesh, you can begin to add
the flowers.

The flowers with strong stems, such as the leucospermum, chrysanthemums and yarrow, can be placed directly into the soaked moss. Wire up the other flowers with double-leg mounts, then arrange all the flowers on both sides of the frame (*right*).

"Decorating hotels usually

requires delicate timing.

Banqueting rooms often have

three changes of occupant in

one day, and fitting in with this

tight schedule frequently means

working with impossible

deadlines and under

extreme pressure."

Groundsheets are essential when decorating hotels and halls because they protect floors from spilled water and stains caused by foliage that has accidentally been trodden underfoot. They also make it much easier to clear up the mess before the reception begins.

Ladders, and sometimes scaffolding frames, are needed for decorating the tall rooms and high ceilings that are often found in churches and ballrooms. An easy way to decorate tall columns is to wind "sausages" of wire mesh and sphagnum moss filled with flowers and foliage around them (*far left*). These can be fixed to the columns using the sort of bolted-ring attachments that are used to hold lights.

CIVIL WEDDINGS

Civil weddings are so quick that bridal parties rarely spend any money on floral

decorations for the ceremony and prefer to decorate the reception party instead.

Nevertheless, little touches, such as buttonholes for all the guests, help

to make the ceremony special.

Above: Buttonholes can be as varied as the imagination. Roses (*Rosa*) continue
to be the most popular and long-lasting flower for weddings. A classic rose
buttonhole is usually trimmed with three leaves.

Right: Instead of a bridal bouquet, a handbag filled with a posy of flowers makes
an interesting alternative. This handbag is in the same fabric as the bridal outfit
and contains 'La Minuet' roses (*Rosa*), lavender (*Lavandula*), sweet peas (*Lathyrus
odoratus*), green dill (*Anethum graveolens*) and *Hypericum* berries.

Civil weddings can be held in all sorts of venues, which provides a tremendous amount of scope when planning the floral decorations. This gives the wedding couple plenty of flexibility to choose everything, and even to write their own ceremony. Often flowers are kept quite informal, but the nature of some hotel venues means an element of formality is required. If you decide upon this type of venue, it is a good idea to arrange to view the room when it is dressed. The hotel banqueting manager will be experienced and very helpful in guiding you when choosing all the details of your wedding. Seemingly small points such as the colour of the tablecloths can alter the mood of a room significantly. Dark tablecloths can dominate, and it is often best to complement these with brightly coloured or white flower arrangements and to avoid pastel shades, which can look insipid.

Most brides would faint if they saw their reception room three hours before the event because the majority of the details are put into place at the last minute. When the reception is over, everything has to be removed. This is obviously a far less rewarding process than the installation!

Centre: If you wish to have a buffet rather than a sit-down meal, one major table arrangement looks more spectacular than several smaller ones, which can become lost among the dishes of food. Fruit and flowers go extremely well together and the fruit can be eaten by your guests later, if you wish.

Top and bottom left: Fruit and vegetables add drama, texture and colour to floral decorations. Here, the colours of the fruit are matched with the summer-flower mixture of sweet peas (*Lathyrus odoratus*), lady's mantle (*Alchemilla mollis*), lisianthus (*Eustoma*), wheat (*Triticum*), *Ixia*, 'Nicole' and 'Little Silver' roses (*Rosa*), scabious (*Scabiosa*) and 'Acapulco' lilies (*Lilium*).

INFORMAL RECEPTIONS

When planning informal receptions, keep the flowers simple. It is best to use containers that suit their surroundings, otherwise they will look out of place or simply like an afterthought.

Above: A blue ceramic bowl filled with moth orchids (*Phalaenopsis*), arum lilies (*Zantedeschia*), bells of Ireland (*Molucella laevis*), globe artichoke (*Cynara scolymus*) flowers and anthurium (*Anthurium*) leaves.

Right: Spires of gladioli (*Gladiolus*), foxtail lilies (*Eremurus*), heliconias (*Heliconia*), 'Confetti' roses (*Rosa*), yarrow (*Achillea millefolium*), 'Shamrock' chrysanthemums (*Chrysanthemum*) and large dock (*Rumex*) leaves, encircled by Areca palm leaves.

TIERED CHOCOLATE CAKE

MATERIALS

Floral decorations
Cotoneaster (*Cotoneaster*)
    berries
Rosemary (*Rosmarinus*)
Viburnum tinus

Cake decorations
Selection of fruit including
    crab apples, kumquats, red
    currants and marrons glacés
Roll of paper towel
3 egg whites
Mixing bowl
Fork
Small brush
4oz (125g) caster sugar
Non-stick silicone paper

Cake
1 round cake, larger than
    the biggest square cake
    (below), set on a cake circle
    and iced with chocolate
    fondant icing
3 square cakes, in descending
    order of size, iced with
    chocolate fondant icing

Optional table garland
Ivy (*Hedera*) trails
Green florist's reel wire
Pearl-headed pins

The bride and groom are the main focus of the wedding, but the cake is often the next big focal point and it is certainly an important part of wedding tradition. Cutting the cake is one of the most photographed rituals of a wedding party.

1 Wash the foliage and berries and leave them to dry thoroughly, to give them a clean, crisp look. Wash the fruit (but not the marrons glacés) and dry it carefully with sheets of paper towel. Separate the red currants into small bunches. Lightly beat the egg whites with the fork in a mixing bowl until they are slightly frothy.

2 Working with one piece of fruit at a time, frost it by brushing it all over with the lightly-beaten egg white until evenly coated and then either sprinkle the fruit with caster sugar or roll it in a bowl of the sugar. Leave the fruit to dry for at least half an hour on non-stick silicone paper. Continue until all the fruit has been frosted.

3 Start to build up the cake. Place the three square cakes, in descending size, on top of the round cake. The rounded shape of the bottom layer allows more room for the decorations. Cut the foliage into small sprigs, taking care to remove any damaged or unattractive pieces.

4 Begin to place the sprigs of foliage and berries on the cake, then add the sugared fruit. Continue until you have decorated all the tiers of the cake. Top the smallest cake with a circle of leaves, berries and fruits.

Optional table garland
You can make a garland for your cake table by binding together trails of ivy with reel wire (preferably green to blend with the colour of the ivy). When the garland is long enough to encircle the table, pin it on using pearl-headed pins. Hide the pin heads beneath the leaves.

TRADITIONAL CAKE

MATERIALS

Hypericum berries

Delicate ivy (*Hedera*) leaves

Sprigs of *Viburnum tinus*

Cream lisianthus (*Eustoma*)

Iceland poppies (*Papaver nudicaule*)

'Unique' roses (*Rosa*)

Florist's knife

Flowerfood solution

1 block of floral foam

3 polystyrene cups

Thin white floral foam tape

Three-tiered iced wedding cake on a cake circle

Florist's reel wire

Poppies (*Papaver*) need very careful conditioning. Most commercial poppies come pre-conditioned with their ends singed and should not be cut. If you do need to cut them, you should reseal their stems yourself. To do this, singe the cut stems with the flame from a candle to prevent sap loss. Alternatively, you can dip the stem ends in boiling water for five seconds to prevent the loss of latex from the stems.

1 Wash the foliage and berries and leave them to dry thoroughly. Cut the flower and foliage stems to a length of about 1½–2½ inches (3.5–6cm) and reseal the poppy stems as described above. Put aside about one third of the flowerheads and ivy leaves, in water, to place around the bottom edge of the cake. Soak the floral foam in a solution of flowerfood (see page 24).

2 Cut off the top of each polystyrene cup, using the florist's knife, to create small containers for the floral foam.

Cut a small piece of floral foam to fit each cup, making it nearly twice as tall as the container so that a trailing arrangement can be created in each. Trim the edges of the foam so that they are curved. Secure the floral foam in the polystyrene cups with the floral foam tape. Arrange the foliage in the cups and trail the ivy over the edge of each cup, making sure that it is not too high, otherwise it will not fit between the cake tiers. Allow more trailing ivy for the top arrangement. Place the cups between the tiers and arrange the flowerheads among the foliage.

3 Bind the stems of the remaining ivy together with florist's reel wire to form a garland for the base of the cake to hide the cake circle. Finally, place the remaining cut flowerheads among the ivy (*right*). If you can, it is best to place all the flowerheads among the foliage just before the reception begins, so that they are in water for as long as possible.

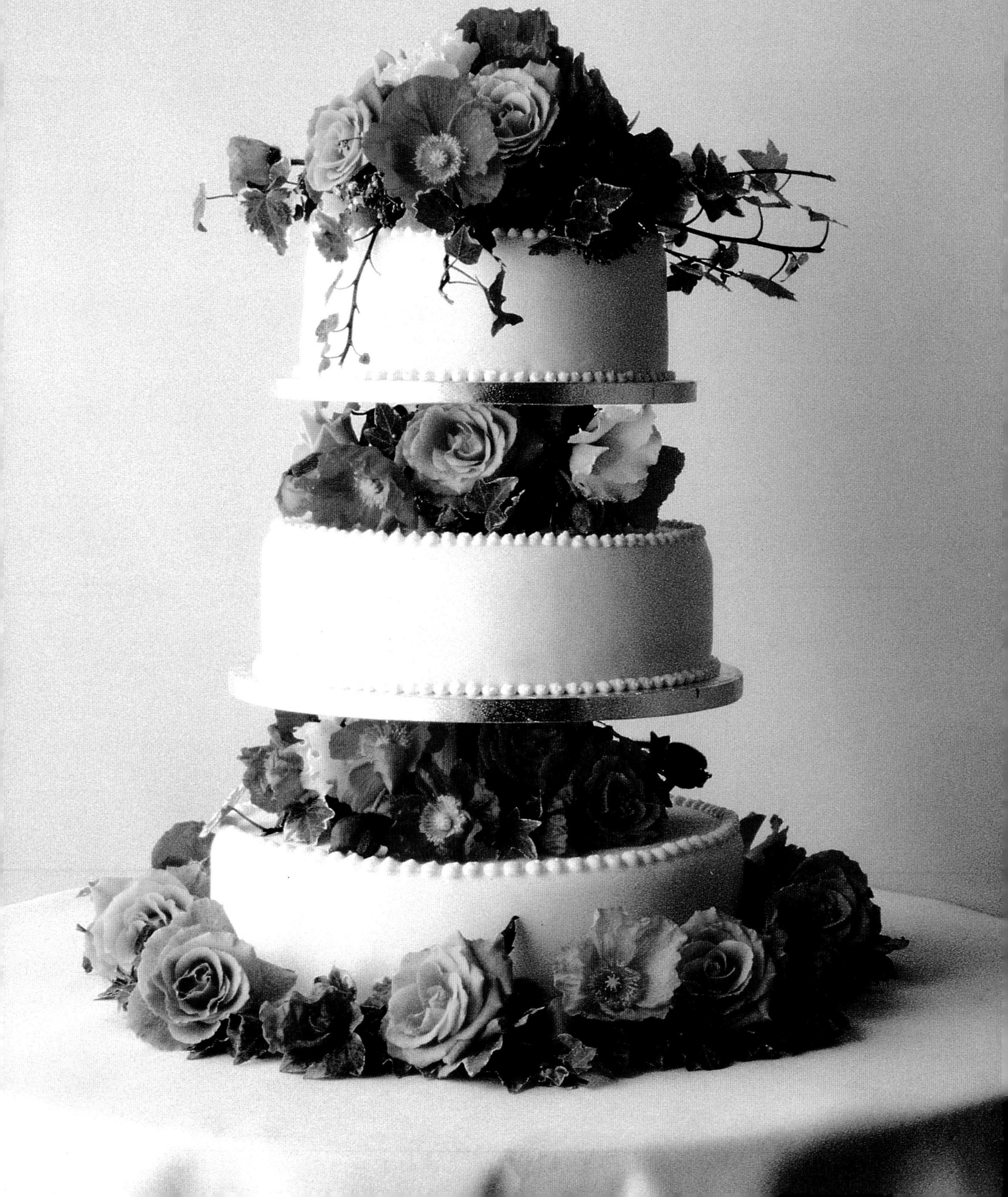

BIRTHS AND

CHRISTENINGS

Don't even think about running your own flower business unless you are a morning person. Flower markets open in the early hours of the morning and are teeming with florists busy buying up that day's stock for their shops. If you like to be ahead of the crowd and if the dawn chorus is your sort of music, this is the perfect occupation.

Some days the choice is overwhelming, especially when I catch my first glimpse of the new season's flowers. When floral inspiration is lacking, I head for the fruit and vegetable section to get some fresh ideas. However, there is never much time to browse because I always have to load the van and get back to the shop before the rush hour begins.

"There is no substitute for

selecting your own raw materials.

Wholesale flower markets the

world over are a great inspiration,

and many of my ideas come from

my early-morning visits to the

London flower market at

New Covent Garden."

CHRISTENING PARTY

Delicate flowers are often the natural choice for christenings or other birth celebrations. Among the blooms that are particularly suitable are snowdrops (*Galanthus*), lily-of-the-valley (*Convallaria majalis*), cowslips (*Primula veris*), spray roses (*Rosa*), grape hyacinths (*Muscari*) and hellebores (*Helleborus*).

Left: Most of the flowers used here are small, delicate and in pastel shades. From top to bottom, they are: a simple arrangement of spray roses (*Rosa*) and lily-of-the-valley (*Convallaria majalis*); camomile (*Chamaemelum nobile*) flowerheads floating in champagne-filled glasses; and hellebores (*Helleborus*), grape hyacinths (*Muscari*) and 'Princess' and 'Diadeen' spray roses next to a conical cake – a perfect alternative to traditional christening cakes.

Right: A bowl of 'Rising Sun' roses (*Rosa*) with only a few leaves makes a striking table decoration. If you feel uncertain about arranging your own flowers, you can take the vase to a florist and have them arranged for you.

NEW ARRIVAL GIFTS FOR MOTHERS

At one time it was fashionable to send blue or pink flowers to mothers to mark

the arrival of either a boy or a girl. Today, however, customers shy away from this

tradition and tend to order something that is bright, cheerful and unisex.

Often floral gifts for the mothers are accompanied by gifts for the baby.

Above: This painted terra-cotta pot has been filled with matching flowers – blue
Agapanthus and lilac hyacinths (*Hyacinthus*) have been mixed with 'Red Velvet',
'Leonotus' and 'Limona' roses (*Rosa*), *Bupleurum*, *Hypericum* berries and
germini (*Gerbera*).

Right: Whenever a new flower variety appears it allows for further
experimentation by the growers. Here, two new roses (*Rosa*), the lilac 'Delilah'
and the lime-yellow 'Limona', have been grouped with clumps of cut papyrus
(*Cyperus papyrus*). Ivy (*Hedera*) leaves trail over the edges of the basket.

BEDSIDE FLOWERS

Bouquets for people in the hospital should be compact, cheerful and robust. Nursing

staff do not have the time to arrange flowers, so it is a good idea to make an

arrangement that sits in its own container. Flowers, whether in vases or arranged in

floral foam, need to be topped up with water daily to combat the dry atmosphere.

Above: A posy of sweet-scented lavender (*Lavandula*), lisianthus (*Eustoma*), lady's
mantle (*Alchemilla mollis*), fresh poppy (*Papaver*) seed heads, sweet Williams
(*Dianthus barbatus*) and red roses (*Rosa*).

Right: One ceramic pot holds cornflowers (*Centaurea*), scabious (*Scabiosa*),
anemones (*Anemone*), viburnum (*Viburnum*) berries and ivy (*Hedera*). In the pink
pot are lisianthus (*Eustoma*), 'Wendy' spray roses (*Rosa*) and green orach (*Atriplex*).

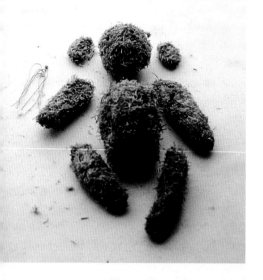
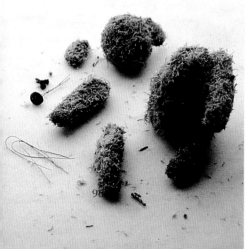

MOSS TEDDY BEAR

MATERIALS

Sphagnum moss
Florist's reel wire
Florist's scissors
Bunch of heavy stub wires
Cloves
Small button
Small wool scarf or length of
    cord or ribbon
Bunch of feverfew (*Matricaria*)

This teddy bear makes an ideal gift and needs neither watering nor special care. If the bear is given as a present to a child who has a new brother or sister, it should be displayed out of the child's reach and not played with, because it contains wires.

1 Work on a flat, non-scratch and waterproof surface, or cover the work surface with plastic sheeting. Roll the moss into four sausage shapes (two small ones for the arms and two large ones for the legs), one round ball for the head, one oval for the body and two tiny sausages that will form the bear's ears.

2 Bind each shape with the reel wire to keep the moss in position. To do this, hold the moss in one hand and, with the other, wind the reel wire around the moss in a clockwise direction. Cut the wire and neatly tuck the ends into the moss.

3 Trim the shapes so that the moss is neat, with no trailing ends, using the florist's scissors. Bend the heavy stub wires double to form hairpins.

4 To assemble the teddy bear, push a wire hairpin through the first leg and attach this to the body by pushing the open ends of the hairpin into the body. Continue this process with the other three limbs, the head and the ears. When you have completed the bear, stick the cloves into his head to make his eyes and attach the button with a stub wire to form his nose (*right*). Tie the scarf or a length of cord or ribbon around his neck. Cut several individual feverfew flowers to make a small bunch and wire this into the bear's paw. Finally, give him a pair of spectacles made by bending a length of reel wire into a suitable shape.

CHRISTENING FLOWERS

Birth celebrations are an excellent opportunity to make the most of seasonal flowers, which are in plentiful supply, to arrange throughout the home. For christening ceremonies, flowers are often put around the base of the font.

Above: The long green stems of the 'Professor Blaauw' irises (*Iris*) help to balance the irises' bright purple with the sharp yellow of the yarrow (*Achillea millefolium*).

Right: Nine belladonna lilies (*Amaryllis belladonna*) have been tied together and then placed in a pot with floral foam. Around the base, further belladonna heads have been mixed with *Eryngium* 'Orion', 'Delilah' roses (*Rosa*), double lisianthus (*Eustoma grandiflorum*) and guelder roses (*Viburnum opulus*).

CHRISTENING TREE

Natural topiary trees are easy to make and very effective. Select seasonal flowers that are inexpensive and plentiful. Look for flowers with strong stems that can support themselves, such as *Narcissus*, *Ranunculus*, sunflowers (*Helianthus*) and roses (*Rosa*).

1 Work on a flat, non-scratch and waterproof surface, or cover the work surface with plastic sheeting. Condition the flowers (see page 20). Soak the floral foam in a solution of flowerfood (see page 24). Cut the floral foam to fit the pot, using the florist's knife, making sure that it is tall enough to sit above the rim. Remove the foam from the pot.

2 Line the terra-cotta pot with the plastic sheet, cutting it to size with the florist's scissors. Fit the floral foam into the pot, trimming it to size if necessary with the knife. Disguise the edges of the foam by pushing pieces of Spanish moss into the space between the foam and the plastic.

3 Remove all the foliage from the yarrow stems with the knife and gently gather the flowerheads in your hand to form a tree-like ball. When you are happy with the shape, use some of the ribbon to tie the stems together just beneath the flowerheads.

4 Use the scissors to trim the stems level to suit the scale of the flowers and the pot. Tie the base of the stems securely together with more ribbon and gently push them into the middle of the floral foam. You may wish to guide them with your hands to prevent the stems from buckling. Finally, arrange more of the Spanish moss over the exposed floral foam until it is completely hidden (*right*).

CHRISTMAS

"Each year I am asked to start

thinking about Christmas in the

middle of the year, so by the time

I get round to planning my own

Christmas decorations I can feel a

little jaded. That is why I enlist

energetic helpers who never seem

to tire of the endless festivities

and always revive my enthusiasm."

There is nothing more romantic than a natural Christmas tree. In recent years there has been a huge public demand for trees that last well and do not shed too many needles. The best way to treat a natural tree is to bring it indoors only for the twelve days of Christmas. The current trend for prolonged festivities does not suit Christmas trees and the use of central heating means that even the longer-lasting large-needle varieties, such as noble fir (*Abies*) and blue spruce (*Picea*), find the extended spells indoors extremely dehydrating. To counteract this, keep your tree watered even if it does not have roots. Flowerfood will also help (the food designed for woody stems is the best choice, mixed in tepid water).

CHRISTMAS DECORATIONS

You can introduce extra texture and colour into your Christmas arrangements with fruits and vegetables. Apples and citrus fruit last well in topiary trees, and glossy vegetables such as capsicums and aubergines look good when wired into a wreath. Dried material such as lichen twigs provide a natural wintery feel.

Above: This wreath of blue spruce (*Picea*) incorporates lichen-covered twigs and simple groups of fruit and vegetables. Clusters of skimmia (*Skimmia*) berries, dried lotus (*Nelumbo nucifera*) seed heads and sliced dried quince add texture.

Right: A topiary tree decoration, containing variegated holly (*Ilex*), pittosporum (*Pittosporum*), *Viburnum tinus*, clusters of dark-blue *Viburnum* berries, red chilies, 'Red Lion' amaryllis (*Hippeastrum*), fruits and curly ting-ting.

Large wreath decorations can be used indoors to create

impact. They are particularly effective for a special party,

when you can decorate them to match your chosen theme.

Any type of evergreen foliage can be used to make

a wreath but my favourite is blue spruce (*Picea*). It lasts

extremely well, is a beautiful silver-gray colour and smells

wonderful. Other long-lasting alternatives include *Cupressus*

and box (*Buxus sempervirens*), although neither has such an

aromatic scent. Before making the wreath, you should

condition the foliage (see page 20). To make the wreath, you

need a wire wreath-frame, which is available from florists, a

carrier bag of moss, some foliage, heavy stub wires and

heavy-gauge florist's reel wire. Using the reel wire, bind the

moss onto the wreath-frame. Wire all the foliage with a

double-leg mount (see page 20). To secure the wired foliage

to the wreath, insert the wire at an angle opposite to the way

you wish to position it. When the wire is inserted, bend the

foliage in the opposite direction to anchor it.

Far left: This large wreath of blue spruce (*Picea*) has been decorated with purple velvet ribbon and gold decorations, including toy trumpets and trombones.

Left, from top to bottom: Mini gold apples have been fashioned from gold-sprayed hollow grasses. Fresh oranges last well in indoor decorations, especially if you choose very firm, slightly under-ripe ones. You can also buy some excellent plastic versions that look extremely authentic. Vines have been wound around a star-shaped frame and then sprayed with gold paint to create Christmas stars.

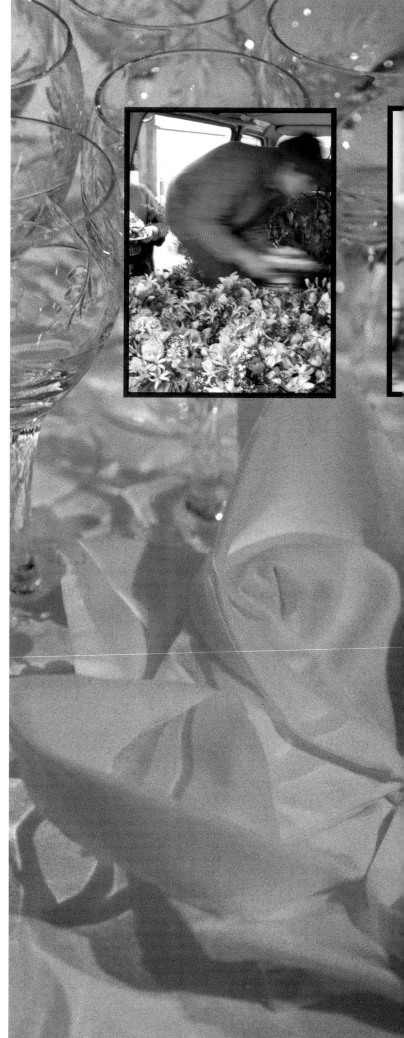

For this corporate Christmas party, gold urns were filled with flowers in concentric circles, in the Victorian fashion, to complement the 19th-century hotel setting. Whenever possible it is always preferable to assemble a large flower arrangement on site, so that it fits the space perfectly in terms of height, shape and size. Balance is very important in large arrangements and when you put one together on site it will be more stable than if it had been transported. It is usually best to make smaller arrangements in advance. Flower arranging is a messy business, and berries in particular can stain carpets and furnishings, so you should always use dust sheets to cover the floors and furniture.

"When you get used to working

with flowers you start to handle

them in a far more robust

manner than when they were

foreign to you, although you

should still treat delicate blooms

with respect."

TABLE DECORATIONS

Decorating the table with seasonal foliage and flowers is an essential part of any

Christmas dinner or buffet. Arrangements can be large and lavish if space allows or

you can simply trim the napkins with ribbons and berries.

Above: For a special Christmas party, napkins can be tied with ribbon and a few
flowers or a sprig of foliage to give a personal touch. Here, gold-sprayed ivy
(*Hedera*) berries and 'Serena' roses (*Rosa*) are tied with a gold-edged silk bow.

Right: Wreath frames, which are available from florists, make a good base for
Christmas table centres. Here, a 10-inch (25cm) diameter wreath frame has been
covered with variegated holly (*Ilex*), *Viburnum tinus*, ivy (*Hedera*) berries, red spray
roses (*Rosa*) and eucalyptus (*Eucalyptus*) pods.

Christmas is a good time to experiment with traditional floral arrangements, especially if you want to give them a new twist or to combine some unusual ingredients. This delicate topiary tree (*right*) would make a wonderful gift. A cluster of cinnamon sticks has been placed in a weathered terra-cotta pot, then a ball of floral foam has been taped on top of the sticks and decorated with hypericum (*Hypericum*) berries, holly (*Ilex*) leaves, gilded pine cones and roses (*Rosa*). To wire a pine cone, wrap a heavy stub wire around the bottom of the cone, then bring the two ends of the wire together and twist them to form a double-leg mount, which can then be inserted in floral foam.

All red-coloured flowers are more expensive at Christmas time because of the great demand. The general shortage of raw material in winter makes this an excellent time for using long-lasting flowers, such as *chrysanthemum*, carnations (*Dianthus*) and *Dendrobium* orchids. You can also gild and silver seed heads and twigs, which retain their shape in warm rooms as they are already dehydrated, and use ribbon and rope decoratively to make up for any lack of floral colour.

Right: Dried flowers and seed heads – Mexican hats and Eucalyptus (*Eucalyptus*) pods – *Vibernum tinus* berries and twisted rope, wired into the base of a topiary tree.

Below: Bright-pink roses (*Rosa*), purple anemones (*Anemone*) and *Hypericum* berries, arranged in a glass tumbler that has been covered in silvered leaves attached using double-sided tape.

Bottom: To spray leaves with silver paint, make sure that they are dry, then place them on a protected surface in a room with good ventilation.

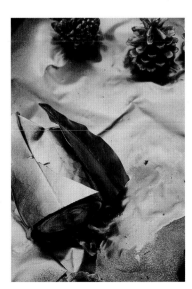

GARLANDS AND WREATHS

The custom of making celebratory garlands and wreaths dates from ancient history. Traditionally, laurel (*Laurus*), olive (*Olea*) and rosemary (*Rosmarinus*) were used; blue pine (*Picea*), cypress (*Cupressus*) and box (*Buxus sempervirens*) are all popular today.

Above: Pine cones and leaves have been sprayed silver to give this garland of blue pine (*Picea*) a subtle "antique" look.

Right: A wreath of fresh flowers, using ivy (*Hedera*) berries, poppy (*Papaver*) seed heads, *Hypericum* berries, *Carthamus*, 'Festival' lilies (*Lilium*), green dill (*Anethum graveolens*), *Cymbidium* and 'Maggie Oei' *Dendrobium* orchids, scabious (*Scabiosa*) seed heads and dahlias (*Dahlia*), with a bow of flax leaves.

HANGING ADVENT RING

MATERIALS

Pink heather plants (*Erica*)

Belladonna lilies (*Amaryllis belladonna*)

'Jacaranda' roses (*Rosa*)

Box (*Buxus sempervirens*)

Cardoons (*Cynara cardunculus*)

Branch of variegated holly (*Ilex*)

Blue pine (*Picea*)

Florist's knife

Flowerfood solution

6 beeswax candles

Bunch of heavy stub wires

Floral foam tape

Sphagnum moss

20-inch (50cm) diameter wire wreath frame

Heavy-gauge florist's reel wire

Florist's scissors

Limes

Pears

Several yards (metres) of 3-inch (7.5cm) wide silk ribbon

Ornamental cabbages (*Brassica oleracea*)

Several yards (metres) of silver cord

Hanging Advent rings do not have to be confined to Christmas and can be an excellent decoration for an autumnal evening party. This Advent wreath was inspired by an order I received in my shop for a decoration for a Burns Night celebration. The clumps of heather have been cut from garden plants and wired into the arrangement.

1 Work on a flat, non-scratch and waterproof surface, or cover the work surface with plastic sheeting. Condition the flowers and foliage (see page 20). Cut down the stems to a length of about 1½–2½ inches (3.5–6cm), ready for wiring, and strip off any lower foliage with the florist's knife. Wire the candles by bending 12 of the stub wires double to form hairpins and taping two of them onto the end of each candle using floral foam tape.

2 Tease out the sphagnum moss and remove any foreign bodies. Wrap handfuls of moss around the wreath frame, binding it tightly in place with the reel wire. Continue until the frame is evenly covered with the moss. When making a hanging Advent wreath you must bind

the moss on either side of the ring so that you can place plant material facing both upward and downward. Once the wreath is nicely rounded, trim off any extra pieces of moss, using the florist's scissors, so that it is smooth and firm. Thread a heavy stub wire through each piece of fruit and then twist the two ends of wire together.

3 Cut the ribbon into three equal lengths and securely tie them to the frame so that you can hang up the wreath. Wire all the flowers, foliage and the ornamental cabbages with double-leg mounts (see page 20). Arrange the foliage around both sides of the wreath.

4 Taking the length of silver cord, pin one end of it into the moss with a stub wire bent double and weave it in and out of the foliage to create a rich effect. Now add the flowers, fruit and cabbages in clusters around the wreath until you are happy with the arrangement. Push the candles, in groups of two, into the wreath, using the pins to hold them firmly in place (*right*). Gather the ends of the ribbons together into a firm bow and hang up the wreath.

SPICE AND FRUIT GARLAND

MATERIALS

Bunch of heavy stub wires

Fir cones

Red apples

Dried orange slices

Gold-sprayed *Canella* berries

Several yards (metres) of red
    velvet ribbon

Scissors

Cinnamon sticks

Gold-sprayed twig bundles

Blue spruce (*Picea*)

Heavy-gauge florist's reel wire

The custom of decorating your house with evergreens at Christmas can be traced back to the Roman festival of Saturnalia (the feast of the birth of the unconquered Sun after the shortest day of the year), as well as to the Norse celebration of the feast of the Winter Solstice, known as Yuletide. Bringing greenery into the house was supposed to provide a retreat for the wood god and goddess from the seasonal chills and storms of winter. This was originally a pagan belief, so for a long time Christians were discouraged from bringing greenery into their households.

1 Work on a flat, non-scratch and waterproof surface, or cover the work surface with plastic sheeting. First, prepare the decorative elements with stub wires. To wire a fir cone, wrap a stub wire around the base and twist the two ends tightly so that the wire does not slip off the cone. To wire the fresh and dried fruit, insert a stub wire through the flesh and twist the ends together. Wire the *Canella* berries with double-leg mounts (see page 20). Make the bows, using about 1 yard (1m) of ribbon for each. Follow the method described on page 134 but, instead of tying the middle with ribbon, wrap a stub wire around the middle and twist it to create two legs of wire. Wire the cinnamon sticks into bundles, then wire these and the bundles of twigs with double-leg mounts.

2 Cut the blue spruce into sprigs 3 inches (7cm) long. To create the garland, place one sprig on top of another and bind them together with reel wire. Build up the garland by adding further bunches, each time securing them with reel wire. Make sure that all the sprigs point in the same direction.

3 When you have completed the garland you can add the embellishments. Place the wire of each ingredient through the pine and twist it back on itself. Cut off any extraneous stub wires at the back of the garland to reduce its weight. Alternate the different types of decoration so that you have a rich, textured look (*right*).

FRUIT AND FOLIAGE ARRANGEMENTS

I love to design floral arrangements in which the base and the content complement one another, and to use alternative natural materials for both. Incorporating fruit in floral arrangements is traditional, as shown in many early still-life paintings.

Above: Cinnamon sticks, glued onto a plastic floral bowl, surround textural dahlias (*Dahlia*), nerines (*Nerine*), freesias (*Freesia*), 'Yellow Success', 'Nicole' and 'Tamango' spray roses (*Rosa*), blue spruce (*Picea*), *Cotoneaster* berries, *Hypericum* berries, *Rudbeckia* and poppy (*Papaver*) seed heads.

Right: Dried moss has been glued onto a plastic base and twigs adorn the edges. Inside are *Fritillaria*, 'Lambada', 'Delilah' and 'Nicole' roses (*Rosa*), pink anemones (*Anemone*), guelder roses (*Viburnum opulus*), aubergines and mangoes.

Rather than have one large arrangement, a number of smaller ones can be used to create a display for a long table. Here, different ceramic pots have been filled with various foliages – *Brunia alopecuroides, Eucalyptus, Hebe, Garrya elliptica, Viburnum tinus* and box (*Buxus sempervirens*).

CANDLE DISPLAY

MATERIALS

'Minerva' amaryllis
    (*Hippeastrum*)
'King' spray roses (*Rosa*)
'Royale' roses
Box (*Buxus sempervirens*)
Green dill (*Anethum*
    graveolens)
Guelder rose berries
    (*Viburnum opulus*)
Variegated holly (*Ilex*)
Hypericum (*Hypericum*) berries
Leucadendron 'Safari Sunset'
Blue pine (*Picea*)
Rosehips
White trachelium (*Trachelium*)
Florist's knife
Flowerfood solution
16-inch (40cm) diameter floral
    foam wreath
Montbretia (*Crocosmia*) seed
    heads
Gold spray paint
Bunch of heavy stub wires
4 beeswax candles
Floral foam tape
Bunch of 12–18-inch
    (30–45cm) green garden
    canes
Clear adhesive tape

This arrangement makes a wonderful display for a dining table and would look equally good on a side table at a Christmas party. The colours follow the traditional red and green Christmas scheme but are softened by the variegated amaryllis and the green dill. Amaryllis are at their best during the Christmas season.

1 Work on a flat, non-scratch and waterproof surface, or cover the work surface with plastic sheeting. Condition the flowers and foliage (see page 20) except for the montbretia. Soak the foam wreath in a solution of flowerfood (see page 24). Using the knife, trim the edges of the foam so that they are curved. Spray the montbretia with the gold paint, in a well-ventilated area.

2 Wire the candles by bending eight stub wires double to form hairpins and taping two of them onto the end of each candle using floral foam tape. Position the four candles, evenly spaced, on the wreath, pushing the wires into the foam. Cut the foliage into sprigs 3 inches (7cm) long, then strip the foliage from the bottom inch (2.5cm), using the florist's knife. Begin to arrange the foliage in groups around each candle.

3 Continue to add the plant material in groups around the candles. Contrast the textures and colours of the leaves and berries as you work your way around the wreath.

4 Cut off the heads of the amaryllis, leaving about 1 inch (2.5cm) of stem, then push a garden cane up the hollow stem of each, to support the flowerhead. Bind the bottom of the stem to the cane with clear adhesive tape. Cut down the rose stems to a length of about 2 inches (5cm). Position the flowers in groups around the wreath. Finally, add the montbretia seed heads at intervals throughout the wreath (*right*).

CHRISTMAS TREES

Topiary Christmas trees make an excellent alternative to living trees. They can be as small or as large as you wish, and you can decorate them to complement the other colours in the room. As the photographs here show, they look good whether they're very simple or highly decorated.

Above: Glossy laurel (*Laurus*) leaves, which retain their firmness as they dry out, have been pinned onto a topiary frame, working from the bottom, using stub wires bent double. You can also use preserved magnolia (*Magnolia*) leaves.

Right: A conical frame has been filled with sphagnum moss, sprigs of blue spruce (*Picea*) have been pushed into the moss and then fruits, twigs, berries, stars and bows have been added.

CHRISTMAS PEAR TREE

MATERIALS

Box (*Buxus sempervirens*)

'Salal' gaultheria (*Gaultheria shallon*)

Berried holly (*Ilex*)

Florist's knife

Flowerfood solution

Terra-cotta pot

Gold spray paint

Small, firm pears

Dry-hard clay

Birch trunk

3 blocks of floral foam

Frame nailed to the birch trunk, or 2 hanging baskets

Heavy-gauge florist's reel wire

Sphagnum moss

1-inch (2.5cm) gauge wire mesh, large enough to cover the floral foam

Bunch of 12–18-inch (30–45cm) green garden canes

Red pomegranates

Small fir cones

For a large topiary tree such as this, it is very important to think about the mechanics, especially if you want the tree to last for two or three weeks. Here, iron rods have been soldered together into a cage to hold three blocks of floral foam, and this has been nailed to the top of the trunk. You could, instead, wire a foam-filled hanging basket on either side of the trunk. If you are putting a lot of heavy plant material into the tree, weight the base with stones or cement.

1 Work on a flat, non-scratch and waterproof surface, or cover the work surface with plastic sheeting. Condition the foliage (see page 20). Begin by covering the terra-cotta pot with gold spray paint. Then spray one side of the pears, leave them to dry, turn them over and spray the other side. Make sure that you work in a well-ventilated room. Fill the pot with the dry-hard clay and firmly push the birch trunk into the middle. Make sure that the trunk stands upright.

2 Soak the blocks of floral foam in a solution of flowerfood (see page 24). Fill the metal frame, or the hanging baskets, with the blocks of floral foam, trimming them to fit using the florist's knife. Attach the hanging baskets, if used, to the top of the trunk and wire the edges of the baskets together to form a sphere, using reel wire. Cover the foam or the baskets with sphagnum moss, leaving some moss aside, and then wrap with the wire mesh. Secure the mesh with reel wire.

3 Cut down the foliage stems to a length of about 2½–3½ inches (6–8.5cm) and remove the lower leaves, using the florist's knife. Establish the shape of the tree by inserting bunches of the box and the 'Salal' gaultheria in the foam.

4 Prepare the fruits by pushing a garden cane into the side of each one – these will hold the fruit in place in the foam. (Cut the canes in half first if they are too long.) Make sure that the cane does not puncture the skin on the other side of the fruit. Alternate the pomegranates and pears around the tree, then arrange the sprigs of holly. Check the tree from all angles to make sure that it has a rounded shape and the fruit and berries are distributed evenly. Put handfuls of moss around the base of the tree and place the fir cones in the moss (*right*).

D E C O R A T I N G
G I F T S

If you want to create unusual decorations for your Christmas gifts you can use all
kinds of foliage and dried material, such as dried slices of orange or quince. Choose
wrapping paper that picks out the tones of the fruit and foliage.

Above: A purple box has been decorated with variegated ivy (*Hedera*), a pine
cone and a slice of dried quince. Secure each ingredient using a hot-glue gun.

Right: Adding a natural sprig of berries to a gift makes it look very special. Here,
sprigs of spruce (*Picea*), berried variegated holly (*Ilex*) and slices of dried quince
have been arranged in a lavish group. Gold cord and gold-flecked wrapping
paper complete the look.

HAND-TIED BOUQUET

MATERIALS
Cymbidium orchid
'Bianca' roses (*Rosa*)
Selection of evergreen foliage
including eucalyptus
(*Eucalyptus*), holly (*Ilex*),
hypericum (*Hypericum*)
berries, ivy (*Hedera*)
berries, leucadendron
'Safari Sunset'
(*Leucadendron*) and hard
ruscus (*Ruscus*)
Grevillea
Florist's knife
Flowerfood solution
Dried gold-sprayed
pomegranates, (available
ready sprayed)
Gold-sprayed curly ting-ting
(available ready sprayed)
String
Florist's scissors
Length of cellophane
Gold-sprayed magnolia
(*Magnolia*) leaves (available
ready sprayed)
Gold wrapping paper
7 feet (2m) of gold tulle ribbon

Keeping flowers in water at all times helps to lengthen their life. When you buy a tied bunch you can ask to have it packed in water, which is called aquapacking. This is useful when taking flowers to a dinner party because the host or hostess may not have time to arrange them at once.

1 Work on a flat, non-scratch and waterproof surface, or cover the work surface with plastic sheeting. Condition the flowers and foliage (see page 20). Prepare the foliage by stripping off the lower leaves and small branches from each stem, using the florist's knife. The pomegranates are sold wired onto long sticks that you may wish to trim.

2 Taking the roses as the central point, place groups of foliage around them, including the *Grevillea*, adding each stem at an angle. Do not to hold the bunch too tightly, so that you can create an evenly domed and informal bouquet. Add sprigs of curly ting-ting and the pomegranates throughout the posy. When you are happy with the shape, bind the stems tightly together with string. Trim the stems level, using the scissors.

3 Make a pouch for the stems from the cellophane and tie it tightly with string at the same binding point that you used before. This will create a bag to which you can add water.

4 Add the *Cymbidium* orchid. Wrap a circle of magnolia leaves around the bouquet, with the glossy surfaces facing outward. Cut the wrapping paper into a large oval and gather it round the base of the leaves. Tie tightly with string at the binding point.

Finally, make a bow. Start at one end of the ribbon and pinch it in two places using the thumb and forefinger of each hand. Transfer the pinched point of the ribbon in your right hand to that of the ribbon in your left hand and hold both points together. Make a total of six loops, all the same size, so that both halves of the bow comprise three loops. Snip the end of the ribbon at an angle after the last loop. Adjust the loops so that the bow is symmetrical and rounded. Tie the short piece of ribbon tightly around the middle of the bow and then adjust the loops again. Tie the ribbon securing the middle of the bow around the stem of the bouquet (*right*).

GIFTS

"When children visit my shop

before Mother's Day they are

encouraged to select their own

flowers, as well as the colour of

the wrapping paper and the bow."

Every Saturday my shop attracts many children who cannot resist the colours of the flowers, but on the day before Mother's Day especially, the average age of my customers falls dramatically. Mother's Day is a well-established festival, but it has only recently become commercialized. The celebration was originally called Mothering Sunday, and it began when children in service were given a day's holiday to gather posies of wildflowers, especially violets, for their mothers. However, the origin of showing appreciation of our mothers began in Ancient Greece, where a special three-day festival was held to honour Cybele, the mother of the gods, when flowers were collected and offered to her.

SIMPLE GIFTS FOR MOTHER'S DAY

Simple displays can look very beautiful and are particularly charming when given by

young children. Many of the flowers that are available at this time of year have a

fresh, innocent look that is suited to this uncomplicated style of arrangement.

Above: Mother's Day falls either in March or in May, depending on the country.
These spring daffodils (*Narcissus*) are sitting in a jar of water that is hidden by the
small carrier bag. Early summer flowers can be chosen for a Mother's Day in May,
and scented flowers are always a popular choice.

Right: Potted plants are gifts that can still be treasured long after Mother's Day is
over. This polyanthus (*Primula*) has been replanted in an old-fashioned French jam
jar and decorated with a small handful of bun moss.

MOTHER'S DAY ARRANGEMENTS

Without being extravagant, *pot et fleur* (two of which are shown, on pages 142 and 145) are long-lasting arrangements, because you can keep the plant once the flowers have bloomed. *Pot et fleur* was a great hit with the Victorians, who even cut holes in their dining tables in order to accommodate pots of ferns together with vases of flowers.

Above: For this *pot et fleur* I have combined groups of orange germini (*Gerbera*), *Achillea*, bead plants (*Nertera granadensis*) and bun moss with 'Bahama' and 'Jacaranda' roses (*Rosa*).

Right: The container on the near right contains yellow marigolds (*Calendula officinalis*) surrounded by *Lachenalia* 'Quadricolor', the central one contains white anemones (*Anemone*) and achillea (*Achillea ptarmica*), and the one on the far right combines 'Soleil d'Or' daffodils (*Narcissus*) and green dill (*Anethum graveolens*).

Above: Anemones (*Anemone*), ranunculus (*Ranunculus*), guelder roses (*Viburnum opulus*),
green dill (*Anethum graveolens*), 'Nicole' roses (*Rosa*) and glossy camellia leaves (*Camellia*)
all vie for attention in this colourful arrangement with beeswax candles.

Right: This *pot et fleur* combines three jasmine plants (*Jasminum*) with 'Delilah' roses (*Rosa*),
arum lilies (*Zantedeschia*), carnations (*Dianthus*), ranunculus (*Ranunculus*) and guelder roses
(*Viburnum opulus*).

MOTHER'S DAY GIFT

MATERIALS

Tied bunch

Blue agapanthus (*Agapanthus*)

Blue hyacinths (*Hyacinthus*)

Yellow ranunculus
'Cappuccino' (*Ranunculus*)

'Bianca' roses (*Rosa*)

Guelder roses (*Viburnum
opulus*)

Ivy (*Hedera*) berries

Viburnum tinus

Florist's knife

Flowerfood solution

String

Carrier

Card carrier gift bag

Double-sided tape or glue gun

Dried Moneta (*Moneta*) leaves

Florist's scissors

Hole punch

Large sheet of cellophane

Tissue paper

I love the way in which leaves complement flowers. From this I developed a penchant for leafed containers, and these have become my trademark. For this arrangement, I have extended the idea further to make a leafed carrier bag to hold a tied bunch – a refreshing change from the usual basket arrangement or wrapped bouquet that is often given on Mother's Day.

1 Work on a flat, non-scratch and waterproof surface, or cover the work surface with plastic sheeting. Condition the flowers and foliage (see page 20) and then begin to make the tied bunch. Remove the foliage from the flower stems, using the florist's knife. Arrange a mixture of all the varieties in your hand, taking one or two stems of each. Bind the stems halfway up using the string. Continue building the arrangement, spiralling the stems and binding at the narrowest point (this should be where you are holding the flowers), until the bunch has an attractive, domed shape.

2 Carefully remove the rope handles and cover the bag with double-sided tape. Stick the Moneta leaves onto the bag with the tips pointing upward. Work from the top to the bottom, overlapping the leaf edges. You can use a glue gun as an alternative to tape, but you must be careful to avoid marking the leaves. Trim the leaves that sit along the edge level with the bottom of the bag, using the scissors.

3 Using the hole punch, make a hole through each of the leaves at the point where the handle holes have been covered. Replace the handles.

4 Take the sheet of cellophane and gather the edges together, forming a bag around the stems of the flowers that then fans out around the flower heads. Once you are happy with the wrapping, tie the cellophane at the same point that you have bound the stems, using the string. You can then carefully add water to the cellophane bag, making sure that there are no leaks. (This is known as "aquapacking".) Put some gently crumpled tissue paper in the bottom of the carrier, for padding, and place the tied bunch inside.

"February 14th is the longest

day in the florist's calendar – I

have often worked through the

night to prepare the orders

taken the day before and then

spent a full day dealing with

last-minute orders."

Speed is of the essence on Valentine's Day, when we process hundreds of orders in the shop. These are not only orders that we have already received, but also requests from personal shoppers and last-minute telephone calls. We always work in teams to get the job done efficiently but, even so, the night before and the day itself are extremely hectic. To save time, we always try to do as much advance preparation as possible, such as tying all the bows. My role often involves checking the quality of each arrangement as it is completed and making sure that the deliveries are running smoothly. In addition to our regular team of drivers we use black London taxis on what is always our busiest day of the year.

VALENTINE'S DAY

The Victorian language of flowers enabled lovers to send flowers with a hidden romantic message. It is a charming custom to revive today, especially for Valentine's Day. For instance, lily-of-the-valley (*Convallaria majalis*) mean "the return of happiness", which is a lovely sentiment for this romantic time of year.

Left and above: On Valentine's Day we are often asked to include all sorts of additional presents such as chocolates, but our most expensive to date has been a diamond engagement ring. Red roses (*Rosa*) are the classic floral symbol of love, but small posies are popular for lovers, as are delicate flowers such as lily-of-the-valley (*Convallaria majalis*) (*top left*) and snowdrops (*Galanthus*) (*bottom left*).

Right: Each year we offer a new idea for Valentine's Day. The one shown here is a huge heart-shaped basket filled with scented flowers.

VALENTINE POSIES

The worldwide demand for red roses on Valentine's Day has an inflationary effect on

their price. If the day would be incomplete without them, you can incorporate a few

red roses into a vibrant arrangement of seasonal flowers such as tulips (*Tulipa*),

hyacinths (*Hyacinthus*) or, my own personal favourite, *Ranunculus*.

Above: A handmade paper bag contains a glass tumbler filled with guelder roses
(*Viburnum opulus*), 'Tamango' spray roses (*Rosa*), forget-me-nots (*Myosotis*) and
Hypericum berries.

Right: This explosion of opulence contains groups of 'Aalsmeer Gold', 'Royale'
and 'Leonotus' roses (*Rosa*) mixed with ivy (*Hedera*) berries and gold-sprayed
coconut matting that allows the bouquet to be self-supporting.

ALTERNATIVE VALENTINES

Valentine's Day does not have to mean red roses (*Rosa*). There are many other flowers and colours to choose from, especially if you want your arrangement to depart entirely from tradition or to make a statement about your own taste and style.

Above: Simple, architectural flowers are very suitable for men. Here, bells of Ireland (*Molucella laevis*), contorted hazel (*Corylus avellana* 'Contorta'), *Phormium tenax*, arum lilies (*Zantedeschia*) and Arabian chincherinchee (*Ornithogalum*) are edged with *Philodendron xanadu* and tied with seagrass.

Right: This wall trophy offers dramatic variations in texture and shape – cock's comb (*Celosia*), 'Renate' roses (*Rosa*) and trails of variegated ivy (*Hedera*).

MAN'S VALENTINE

MATERIALS
Crimson arum lilies
   (*Zantedeschia*)
Anthurium 'Choco'
Craspedia (*Craspedia globosa*)
Hebe (*Hebe*)
Glory lilies (*Gloriosa superba*)
'Yellow Success' roses (*Rosa*)
Anthurium (*Anthurium*) leaves
Papyrus (*Cyperus papyrus*)
Florist's knife
Flowerfood solution
Length of raffia or plastic tie
Florist's scissors
Cellophane for aquapacking,
   if desired

The practice of sending flowers to men has been growing rapidly in popularity during the past few years. When choosing flowers for a man, it is usually best to look for bold colours, strong architectural shapes and plenty of interest. This arrangement combines the romance of the roses with the exotic quality of the glory lilies, anthuriums and arum lilies.

1 Work on a flat, non-scratch and waterproof surface, or cover the work surface with plastic sheeting. Condition the flowers and foliage (see page 20). Remove the foliage from the lower parts of the stems, using the florist's knife. Cut the hebe into small clumps. Trim the papyrus of any brown or black spikes and cut off the top to give a sharp, clean edge.

2 Group the flowers in threes or sizeable bunches of each variety. Gather together three roses to form the middle of the bouquet, then start to place the groups of flowers around the central roses. As you do so, spiral the stems so that the flowers fan out in an attractive, rounded shape.

3 The flowers have been chosen for their sensual and textured appearance, so continue to build up the plant material in this patchwork fashion. Arrange the flowers so that some sit lower in the bouquet than others to create extra interest. Place the trailing glory lilies around the edge and use the velvety-textured anthurium leaves to trim the bouquet. When you are happy with the look of the bouquet, tie a length of raffia or a plastic tie around the binding point.

4 Hand-tied bouquets are often designed to fit into a vase, so you should trim the bottom of the stems level, ready for arranging, using the florist's scissors. If you will be delivering the bouquet by hand, you may wish to aquapack it (see page 134) to make sure that the flowers remain in good condition until the time comes when they can be arranged in a suitable container (*right*).

BIRTHDAY BOUQUETS

If you can't decide what to buy someone for their birthday, a bouquet of flowers

makes a wonderful gift. Choose blooms that you know are the recipient's favourites,

or design an arrangement that reflects their personality and taste.

Above: This textural basket arrangement has been designed for someone with
Scottish links. Upright sprigs of heather (*Erica*) have been glued to a green
container filled with ivy (*Hedera*) berries, *Eryngium*, 'Delilah' roses (*Rosa*),
cock's comb (*Celosia*), dahlias (*Dahlia*) and arum lilies (*Zantedeschia*).

Right: I love mixing dahlias (*Dahlia*) together for a glorious burst of colour. These
have been wrapped in banana leaves, available from fruit and vegetable markets.

BIRTHDAY ARRANGEMENT

MATERIALS

Curacuma

Crimson arum lilies
 (*Zantedeschia*)

Green love-lies-bleeding
 (*Amaranthus caudatus*
 'Viridis')

Angelica (*Angelica*) seed
 heads

Sea holly (*Eryngium*)

Florist's knife

Flowerfood solution

10-inch (25cm) diameter
 floral foam wreath

10-inch (25cm) wide heavy
 glass vase

Selection of large pebbles

Kiwi vine

This arrangement would make a very unusual birthday gift. The accent is on architectural flowers and foliage, and the twisted kiwi vine links the *Curacuma* with the rest of the arrangement.

1 Work on a flat, non-scratch and waterproof surface, or cover the work surface with plastic sheeting. Condition the flowers and foliage (see page 20). Soak the floral foam wreath in a solution of flowerfood (see page 24). Using the florist's knife, trim the edges of the foam so that they are curved.

2 Fill the vase with pebbles but leave some room in the middle for the flowers. Place the wreath frame on the rim of the vase. Arrange the

Curacuma in the vase through the middle of the wreath frame so that the pebbles hide the stems. Fill the glass with water.

3 Cut down the stems of the flowers, the sea holly and the angelica seed heads to a length of about 2½ inches (6cm), using the florist's knife, and begin to arrange them in groups around the wreath frame. Leave enough space between the wreath flowers and the *Curacuma* so that you can clearly see the lines of this beautiful flower. Continue to add flowers around the wreath (*right*), making sure that the trails of love-lies-bleeding and the other plant material hide the plastic rim of the wreath frame. Finally, add a few sprigs of kiwi vine to give movement to the arrangement.

INDEXES

GENERAL INDEX

LATIN INDEX

ACKNOWLEDGMENTS

I would like to thank all the people who have contributed to the making of this book, many of whom I am unable to mention in these few lines, and would particularly like to express my gratitude to the following people and organizations.

It has been a joy to work with such a talented photographer as Jonathan Lovekin, who has taken so many astonishingly beautiful photographs for the book during the course of the last year. He has taken far more photographs than could be done justice to in a single book and has been extremely patient, particularly when following my flower-arranging team around Britain. I am also grateful to Jared Fowler and Simon Walton for their assistance with, and enthusiasm for, the project.

I would like to give special recognition to my editor, Jane Struthers, and to thank Judith More, Janis Utton and Anthea Snow at Mitchell Beazley, and Nigel Wright and Beverley Speight at XAB Design.

My suppliers have, as with my earlier books, been very helpful. Thank you to everyone at New Covent Garden Market, and particularly to Dennis Edwards and the team at John Austin & Co. Ltd – they have been most supportive. Dennis's day-to-day contribution to the smooth running of Paula Pryke Flowers is immeasurable and I am sincerely grateful to him, and to David, Lee and all the staff. The success or failure of any business depends upon its staff, and I must express my appreciation of Ashleigh Hopkins, my manager, and of Michelle Geary, who are essential to the efficiency of my company. I would also like to thank the Paula Pryke Flowers team: Joan Cardoza, Melissa Clayton, Jo Dight, Loraine Gilder, Jane Graham, Sam Griffiths, Jane Houghton, Abbigail Madden, Tania Newman, Ann Pochetty, Chris Sharples, Sonia Tomlinson, Liz Wickendon, Leanne Zenonos, John Barry, Glenn McCullough, Patrick Delaney, Moira Seedhouse, Tracy Sedgwick, Jane Barber, Tina Barber, Emma Brown, Angela Chamberlain, Sam Davis, Anita Everard, Carole Ann Richards, Janet Bremner, Shinako Atsumi, Tomoko Kojima, Annie Goss, Sarah Jackson and Michelle O'Connor – and to give a special thanks to Gina Jay.

I must also thank the many clients and friends who have made this book possible and to whom it is dedicated: The Berkeley Hotel, Madeline and Charlie Birchmore, Sir Terence Conran, Dean Gibson, Harkness Roses, Nigel and Mary Houghton, Celia Keyworth (for the food shown on pages 32–3), Konditor and Cook (for the innovative cake shown on page 90), The Lanesborough Hotel, The Landmark Hotel, Le Pont de la Tour, Sanjana and Lily Lovekin, Lucy Miller, Knud Nielson, The New West End Synagogue, Dennis and Liza Pochetty, Katie, Hayley and Thomas Pryke, Helene and Michael Rothschild, Sadlers Wells, Mr and Mrs Spedding and family, Neil Stevens, Thornham Parva Church, Well Heck Pottery.

Last, but by no means least, I would like to thank my parents and my husband, Peter.

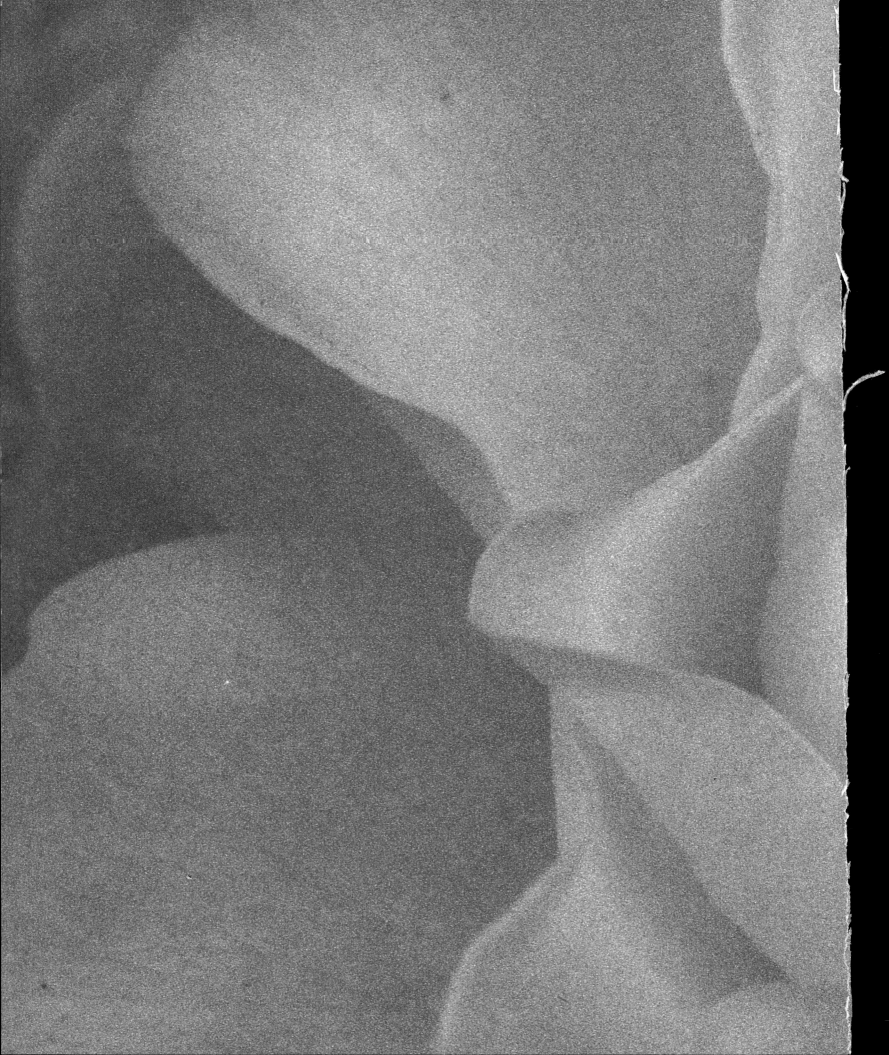